Bitita's Diary

Latin American Realities

Robert M. Levine, Series Editor

BITITA'S DIARY
The Childhood Memoirs of Carolina Maria de Jesus
Carolina Maria de Jesus, Author
Robert M. Levine, Editor
Emanuelle Oliveira and Beth Joan Vinkler, Translators

POLITICS AND EDUCATION IN ARGENTINA, 1946–1962
Mónica Esti Rein

AFRO-BRAZILIAN CULTURE AND POLITICS
Bahia, 1790s-1990s
Hendrik Kraay, Editor

FIGHTING SLAVERY IN THE CARIBBEAN
The Life and Times of a British Family in Nineteenth-Century Havana
Luis Martínez-Fernández

PILLAGING THE EMPIRE
Piracy in the Americas, 1500–1750
Kris Lane

THE SWEAT OF THEIR BROW
A History of Work in Latin America
David McCreery
(forthcoming)

THE SWORD OF HUNGER
A Latin American History
Roberta Delson and Robert M. Levine
(forthcoming)

Bitita's Diary

The Childhood Memoirs of Carolina Maria de Jesus

Carolina Maria de Jesus

Editor
Robert M. Levine

Translators
Emanuelle Oliveira and Beth Joan Vinkler

M.E. Sharpe
Armonk, New York
London, England

Library of Congress Cataloging-in-Publication Data

Jesus, Carolina Maria de.
[Journal de Bitita. English]
Bitita's diary : the childhood memoirs of Carolina Maria de Jesus / Carolina Maria de
Jesus, author; Robert M. Levine, editor; Emanuelle Oliveira
and Beth Joan Vinkler, translators.
p.   cm. — (Latin American realities)
ISBN 0-7656-0211-3 (hardcover : alk. paper).—ISBN 0-7656-0212-1 (pbk. : alk. paper)
1. Jesus, Carolina Maria de—Childhood and youth. 2. Blacks—Brazil—Social conditions.
3. Poor—Brazil—Social life and customs. 4. Brazil—Rural conditions.
5. Brazil—Social life and customs. 6. Brazil—Race relations.
7. Blacks—Brazil—Biography. 8. Brazil—Biography.
I. Levine, Robert M.   II. Oliveira, Emanuelle.   III. Vinkler, Beth Joan.
IV. Title.   V. Series.
F2659.N4J47   1997
981'.00496'0092—dc21
[B] 97-26341
CIP

Printed in the United States of America

BM (c)   10   9   8   7   6   5   4   3   2   1
BM (p)   10   9   8   7   6   5   4   3   2

Robert M. Levine: To David

Emanuelle Oliveira: To my parents

Beth Vinkler: To Jerry, who knows, with all my love, and to Katie, Matthew, and Jackie, my most valuable gifts, my most important work

Contents

Series Foreword by Robert M. Levine   ix
Acknowledgments   xi
Introduction by Robert M. Levine   xiii

Bitita's Diary

1. Childhood   3

2. The Godmothers   8

3. The Holiday   13

4. Being Poor   17

5. A Little History   26

6. The Blacks   39

7. My Family   46

8. The City   63

9. My Son-in-Law   74

10. Grandfather's Death   79

11. School   90

12. The Farm   95

13. I Return to the City   102

14. The Domestic   105

15. Illness   110

16. The Revolution   114

17. The Rules of Hospitality   120

18. Culture   132

19. The Safe   137

20. The Medium   140

21. The Mistress   143

22. Being a Cook   146

Afterword   153
About the Editor   165

Foreword

The Latin American Realities series presents aspects of life not usually covered in standard histories that tell the stories of governments, economic development, and institutions. Books in this series dwell on different facets of life, equally important, but not often analyzed or described. How have underground economies worked? What strategies have poor people employed to cope with hardship and to improve their lives? How have government policies impacted everyday life? What has been the importance of popular culture? How have members of minority or disadvantaged peoples in Latin America—blacks, recent immigrants, indigenous peoples, men and women of intermediate racial status—fared? How have social and economic changes affected them?

Several types of books are featured in this series. Some of the books provide an overview of important themes—work, hunger, smuggling and piracy, racism, religion, politics—over time and across national boundaries. Others are case studies of a state or region, memoirs, and family life. All of the books bring to their readers fresh historical insights and ways of seeing historical themes rarely incorporated into traditional history books about Latin America.

Bitita's Diary, the autobiographical memoir of the black Brazilian author Carolina Maria de Jesus (1915–1977), reveals details about a world virtually unknown to contemporary educated Brazilians. Bitita

(Carolina's nickname as a young girl growing up in rural Minas Gerais) faced appalling obstacles. What she faced as an impoverished, illiterate black child and young woman, and how she survived to ultimately better her life, is both telling and inspirational. Her memoir, ably translated by Emanuelle Oliveira and Beth Joan Vinkler, stands as one of the most compelling testimonies about race, class, status, and gender ever written about rural Latin America in the early twentieth century.

Robert M. Levine

Acknowledgments

This English-language edition of Carolina Maria de Jesus's *Diário de Bitita* could not have been translated and published without the imaginative cooperation between each of the translators, Emanuelle Oliveira of UCLA and Beth Vinkler of Benedictine University, and the strong support of editor Steve Dalphin. As always, José Carlos Sebe Bom Meihy helped in innumerable ways. This book is part of what may be called the "Carolina Maria de Jesus project," our effort to make available to this generation of readers all of Carolina's writings, including her poetry, plays, short stories, and novels. All of Carolina's unedited writing will be available on microfilm within a few years, and all royalties from sales of books about Carolina as part of this project, including our translated *Bitita's Diary,* go directly to Carolina's grandchildren.

I also thank Nélida Piñón, the president of the Brazilian Academy of Letters, for her assistance behind the scenes. Cristina Merhtens, Elza Rezende, and Quélia Quaresma also aided the project. Thanks also go to my professional colleagues who have lent encouragement to the effort to make Carolina de Jesus's works more widely available and appreciated—especially H. Craig Hendricks, Tim Power, and Jeffrey Lesser. I personally thank Vera Eunice de Jesus Lima, and promise that someday we will bring a copy of this book to Sacramento, where local authorities now honor the woman who during an earlier time was driven from the city in hopelessness, seeking a better life.

Emanuelle thanks Mori Morrison of the UCLA Dean's Office for reading her manuscript, and the Conselho Nacional de Desenvolvimento Científico e Tecnológico (CNPq-Brasil) for providing support for her research and study in the United States. Beth wishes to express her gratitude to the Abbey Endowment Fund of St. Procopius Abbey, Lisle, Illinois, for a generous grant that allowed her to travel to São Paulo in the summer of 1996, where she completed the first version of the translation and did preliminary background research. She also wishes to thank Paula Dempsey for her enthusiasm for the project and for reading early drafts of the first chapters. She adds:

"My gratitude also goes to my colleagues at Benedictine University for encouraging me to pursue the translation. I particularly thank Joan Hopkins, Kodjo Yeboah-Sampong, and Vince Gaddis for their input. Finally, I am especially grateful to Carolina herself, whose story and storytelling made the work enthralling from beginning to end."

Introduction

Of the tens of millions of Brazilian descendants of African slaves, only one, Carolina Maria de Jesus, ever wrote and published about her life. Briefly famous when she was discovered by a newspaperman, who first serialized and then published in book form her diary entries, she died in nearly the same obscurity as she had lived, struggling to raise her children in an urban shantytown (*favela*), and living by scavenging in the trash of the city's streets.

Carolina was born in 1915 in Sacramento, a small, provincial city in the southern part of the state of Minas Gerais, near the border of adjacent São Paulo State. Like most places in the interior, Sacramento's social code placed whites at the top, mixed-race *mulatos* in the middle, and blacks at the very bottom of the status ladder. Like most of Minas Gerais, Roman Catholicism in Sacramento was very pronounced. Residents not in conformity with the expectations of the Church were ostracized. As a result, at birth, Carolina was cursed in multiple ways: for her skin color, her origins—she was the granddaughter of slaves, for her poverty, and for having been born illegitimate. In Sacramento's only Roman Catholic church, during Carolina's childhood and even for several decades thereafter, blacks were not permitted to worship alongside whites.

Technically, Carolina was of mixed-race origin. As she explained in *Bitita's Diary,* her grandmother had been a black woman with straight

Residence of two poor families, interior of São Paulo State, c. 1932.
(Robert M. Levine collection.)

hair, the daughter of a white man. In the United States, this (or even a
far smaller percentage of African ancestry) would have made her
"black"; in Brazil, even one white ancestor as far removed as one's
great great grandmother was enough to allow one to claim *mulato*
status. But in Carolina's case, this was not accepted; her poverty,
illegitimacy, and ebony skin relegated her to the low status of a *preta*
(black woman), and even her relatives, most of whom were *mulatos,*
rejected her. She was raised as a pariah even though she showed keen
intelligence; later, when she was given the opportunity to attend school
for two years, she developed a love of reading that would transform
her life. But she had to be pulled out of school when her mother found
work on a farm; there, Carolina came to love the countryside and the
pastoral life even though her family was forced to work under degrad-
ing conditions and was ultimately cheated out of its wages. The ability
to see good in the midst of suffering characterized her personality. This
optimistic side, in fact, nurtured her and kept her going, and it made
her introspective writing more interesting than had she emphasized the
bitter disappointments of her life.

When her mother died, Carolina decided to leave Sacramento in
search of work as a domestic in larger cities. She ended up in São

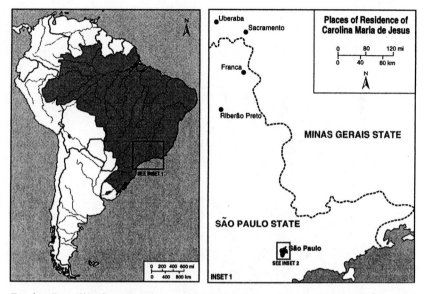

Paulo, Brazil's largest city and burgeoning industrial and commercial center. Economic opportunities for single black women were limited to two: she could sell her body, or she could become a domestic servant. Although Carolina was handsome and considered sexually attractive by men, her internal sense of self-esteem, which somehow had survived years of deprivation, kept her from prostitution. Her road was difficult, and along the way she received only disappointment and scorn. She lived or worked for periods of time in Araxá, Uberaba, Uberabinha, Santos, Ribeirão Preto, and Campinas before arriving in the city of São Paulo where, for migrants from the hinterland, opportunities for employment were greatest even if the streets were not paved with gold.

It is telling that when she arrived in São Paulo Carolina succeeded where most other rural migrants failed: she won a series of jobs as a maid for wealthy families and, as a result, was able to live (if in tiny maid's quarters) in comfortable places and to have access to books and newspapers. At some of her jobs she talked about politics and current events with the masters of the house, who, when they found out how intelligent she was, treated her, over the kitchen table, with intellectual respect. But she could not overcome the way things were, even though she worked in the houses of some the most enlightened individuals in São Paulo—Euricledes Zerbini, a famous heart surgeon; General Pedro

Carolina Maria de Jesus and son João, c. 1949. *(Courtesy Vera Eunice de Jesus Lima.)*

Aurélio Góes Monteiro, a powerful figure in national life; and others.

Sexually active during her rare time off from work, Carolina became pregnant, and, as a potential burden to her employers, was summarily fired. She ended up in Canindé favela, a new and relatively small shantytown whose residents, including Carolina, constructed their shacks out of stolen boards and pieces of tin and other junk. Canindé sat on the banks of the Tietê River, which overflowed its banks every year during the rainy season and drove the residents to seek higher ground; sometimes the winter floods destroyed the shacks and forced the residents to start over again. Life in this world was harrowing, although the fact that São Paulo had far fewer favelas than its sister city, Rio de Janeiro, in the 1950s meant that municipal and

Carolina in Canindé favela at time her first diary was being prepared for publication, 1958. *(Courtesy Vera Eunice de Jesus Lima.)*

charitable agencies were able to provide some aid—handouts of food and clothing, some health care, a nearby police kiosk for protection, school for children—assistance that *favelados* in later decades would not have. Carolina's family, for example, was visited by a social worker, and some of the men (all of them white and foreign-born) who fathered her four children (one of whom died stillborn) gave her money from time to time.

Still, she spent most of each day wandering through the streets with a sack on her head and her children on her back and at her side, collecting trash. When there was no food, they often ate what they could from the garbage. She knew hunger, and was terrified that her children would take sick and die. Men tried to rape her daughter Vera; her sons, João and José Carlos, developed aggressive personalities, stole, and were threatened by adults, one of whom ran after José Carlos with a knife; when Carolina tried to defend him, the attacking woman stabbed her and sent her to the hospital.

What preserved her mental health, and what brought her to the attention of the world, were her diary entries, written each night in her shack on foraged scraps of paper that she sewed into notebooks. She started to write down her daily experiences in 1955, as well as writing poems, short stories, and fragments of plays and novels. In 1958, during an election campaign for mayor of São Paulo, a newspaperman, Audálio Dantas, visited Canindé favela to write a story and discovered that Carolina was keeping a diary. This was during a brief period of reformism in Brazilian politics, and the reporter sensed that readers might be intrigued by the comments of a black *favelada* about her life. He printed them, heavily edited to delete repetition (and to tone down her sarcasm and her willingness to name names when she witnessed corruption or laziness or incompetence), in his afternoon newspaper. When readers responded as he hoped they would, Dantas attempted to edit the diaries further into book form and to find a publisher. After several rejections, he found one—Editora Francisco Alves, one of the country's oldest and most prestigious publishing houses—willing to take a chance on a book written by an unknown in a market where the status of authors was always paramount. When the book was published, in 1960, its success exceeded even Dantas's hopes. Within days it became a runaway best-seller, limited in sales only by the fact that so many thousands of copies were manufactured that the metal plates used in the printing process warped. The author of *Quarto de Despejo,* the title given to the diary, suddenly became a media celebrity. This had a dark side: Carolina herself drew the attention, as if she were a sideshow freak, a scavenger for trash who wrote about life. Only a small portion of the attention given her dwelt on the content of what she wrote, about the social ills that kept people in favelas, about racial discrimination, about strategies for survival among those condemned to lives of misery.

The diary became Brazil's best-selling book, selling more copies than even the picaresque novels of Jorge Amado. Foreign publishers translated the diary: within a few years it appeared in fifteen languages and in more than forty countries, becoming the most widely read book about Brazil ever written. If in Brazil, Carolina's celebrity derived from who she was rather than what she wrote, abroad she was lauded as an eloquent spokesperson for the ills of Third World poverty. Her diary appeared at the height of the Cold War: in North America and Western Europe it was considered a cry for help, a justification for economic aid to Latin America, a rationale for President John F. Kennedy's Alliance for Progress. In the Eastern bloc, where the book became equally popular, it was cited as evidence of the depravity of life under capitalism, a call for social justice. Carolina Maria de Jesus became a phenomenon unprecedented in the annals of publishing, a meteor in the contested skies between East and West.

The full story of Carolina's rise and fall is told in a number of articles and books published in the last few years by members of a research team who set out to find Carolina's surviving children and to interview those who had helped her during her days of fame.[1] Carolina received enough money in royalties to permit her to leave the favela and to buy a sturdy house in a lower-middle-class neighborhood, but she spent all of her money (she was a soft touch for those who approached her in need) and was rejected by her new neighbors because of the commotion she caused in the neighborhood and because she was a black single mother from a favela whose children used foul language and whose blackness offended them. She received very little money from foreign royalties, because the translation rights to her book had been sold on speculation before the book became famous, and no one could have anticipated its remarkable success. All of the editions of her diary published in the communist world were pirated, as was East bloc practice, so she received no royalties at all from East Germany, Hungary, the Soviet Union, Cuba, and the other Soviet satellites.

It did not take her long to realize that attempting to live in a middle-class neighborhood was not viable. In 1970, Carolina sold her house and moved to the outskirts of São Paulo, where she bought a piece of land and built with her own hands a small house of cinder blocks. She chose a location far from the city because it reminded her of her days on the farm outside of Sacramento. She had solitude there, could grow food and raise chickens, and her children could complete their schooling. There, in the district of Parelheiros, she lived forgotten, at first so destitute that she had to ride the bus back to the city with her sack to

---

1. See Robert M. Levine and José Carlos Sebe Bom Meihy, *Cinderela Negra* (Rio de Janeiro: Editora UFRJ, 1994); *The Life and Death of Carolina Maria de Jesus* (Albuquerque: University of New Mexico Press, 1995); *Antologia Pessoal* (Rio de Janeiro: Editora UFRJ, 1996); Andrea Paula dos Santos, *Ponto de Vida* (São Paulo: Edicões Loyola, 1996); Robert M. Levine and Melvin Arrington, Jr., *I'm Going to Have a Little House: The Second Diary of Carolina Maria de Jesus* (Lincoln: University of Nebraska Press, 1997); and José Carlos Sebe Bom Meihy and Robert M. Levine, *Meu Estranho Diário* (São Paulo: Editora Xamã, 1996).

Carolina outside her house in Parelheiros at the time she was writing
Diário de Bitita, **c. 1975.** *(Courtesy* Arquivo do Estado de São Paulo.*)*

scavenge in her old neighborhoods, but ultimately in conditions removed from abject favela misery yet by any standard lacking in any
luxury. When she died in 1977, her obituaries blamed her for failing to
take advantage of the opportunities offered to her by her discovery, an
allusion to the fact that she had never shed her feisty personality and
learned to mimic the manners of her betters. Reporters sent to interview her during her last years in Parelheiros mocked her for her
shabby clothing, the dusty condition of her plot of ground, and for the
fact that she did not even have copies of the Brazilian edition of her
work in her house.

In keeping with her self-disciplined habits, Carolina not only continued to write, but in the years after her sudden fame she published
several more books. Dantas himself put together her second published
diary, *Casa de Alvenaria* (1961), a sequel to *Quarto de Despejo,* following her departure from the favela to her unhappy life in the house
she had bought. This book received scant attention from critics and
was not economically successful. She then used her royalty money to

publish on her own two additional books, *Pedaços da Fome* (1963), and *Provérbios* (1965). She also wrote plays, novels, and short stories, but with the exception of one short story published in an Argentine magazine and a poem published in a São Paulo newspaper, none appeared in print. One of the novels was about her grandfather—*O Escravo* (The Slave)—but it never was accepted by any publisher. José Carlos, her son, later said that Carolina mailed the manuscript to an American editor but never received a reply.

Pedaços da Fome (Pieces of Hunger) dwelled on social issues. In it Carolina wrote about the evils of materialism and society's insistence on judging people on the basis of their background and refinement—sociologists would term this *adscription*. She chastised Brazilian males, depicting them as vain and malevolent. Always morally righteous, she criticized lower-class men for their behavior; she never excused what she considered to be sloth or greed or unreliability on the grounds of poverty's influence. Publishers, then, knew that her books would never find an audience, and they considered her writing crude and unliterary.

Unable to convince even her original publisher to do any more of her books, Carolina turned to a less prestigious press, São Paulo's Editora Aquila. Her new publisher tried everything to make the book succeed, but without any luck. The cover featured a drawing of a poor young girl holding an infant: both seemed to be more Caucasian than black. The introduction was written by Brazilian poet Eduardo de Oliveira and there were four pages of critics' excerpts extolling Carolina's diary, *Quarto de Despejo*.[2] By this time, Carolina had lost her aura of novelty, and few if any reviews of her new writing appeared in the press. Even reminders of her past fame did little to convince intellectuals, who comprised almost the entire market for books, to purchase anything more that she wrote.

No publishing firm was willing to take her fourth manuscript, *Provérbios,* a collection of pearls of wisdom and homespun homilies, so in 1965 she paid for it to be published out of her other royalties.[3]

---

2. Robert M. Levine and José Carlos Sebe Bom Meihy, *The Life and Death of Carolina Maria de Jesus,* 74.

3. Carolina Maria de Jesus, *Provérbios* (São Paulo: Gráfica Editora Luzes, Ltda., 1965). See Melvin S. Arrington, Jr., "Gnomic Literature from the *Favela:* The *Provérbios* of Carolina Maria de Jesus," *Romance Notes* 34:1 (1993), 79–85.

The book was awkwardly written and not very original. Its reception may also have been injured by the fact that it appeared in the second year of Brazil's military dictatorship, a dour period marked by social tension. *Provérbios* was ignored in the press without further comment as the work of "Carolina Maria de Jesus, writer from the favela."[4] There was no women's movement to champion her, nor was there any broad-based movement acknowledging the importance of Afro-Brazilian writing and its perspective. Left-wing intellectuals had their hands full with the dictatorship, and few of them had praised Carolina because she seemed too socially conservative for them, and too centered on her own family, a focus they considered selfish.

In 1982, five years after Carolina's death, Editions A.M. Metailie, a leading French publishing firm located in Paris, published Carolina's fifth and last book.[5] It had been pieced together and translated from manuscript fragments she had given to French reporters who had come to interview her in the house she had built by herself in Parelheiros. Although a Spanish-language translation was later published in Madrid by Ediciones Alfaguara, S.A., no Brazilian publisher showed interest until 1986, when Nova Fronteira, an important publishing house in Rio de Janeiro owned by the Lacerda family, purchased the publication rights from A.M. Metailie and published the book in its original Portuguese as *Diário de Bitita*. *Bitita*, a reference to her childhood nickname, received virtually no critical notice in the Brazilian press or in academic circles.

About the Translation

Carolina Maria de Jesus wrote the short chapters that comprise this autobiography during the early 1970s. By then, the media frenzy that had enveloped her life had long subsided; she continued to live with her children, who by now were in their twenties, on the periphery of the city of São Paulo in the cinder-block house she had constructed practically with her bare hands. She lived the life of a hermit, squabbling with her neighbors and undergoing long periods of silence. It is likely that by this time she was suffering from clinical depression, although since she never had access to medical treatment it is impossi-

---

4. *O Globo* (Rio de Janeiro), December 11, 1969, Arq. *O Globo*.
5. Carolina Maria de Jesus, *Journal de Bitita* (Paris: Editions A.M. Metailie, 1982), 235 pp.

ble to know for sure what ailed her. In fact, when she died in 1977, newspapers reported that she had succumbed to emphysema, although her daughter Vera insisted years later that she never had suffered from breathing disorders, so the cause of her death remains a mystery.

It seems inevitable that under these circumstances, and given the fact that she wrote her memoirs at a point near the end of her life, some of the content in *Bitita's Diary* may be inaccurate. Carolina had a sharp memory and an ability to recall detail, but she sometimes got dates and names wrong as well as prices of things.

Such errors, however, are remarkably minor for a book written under such difficult circumstances, at the end of a life rooted in misery interspersed by a short, unmanageable phase of celebrity. Carolina de Jesus's childhood memoirs comprise the best and most precise glimpse into the world of rural Brazilian life in the 1920s and 1930s that has ever been written. What she tells us about her pariah status, about animosities between blacks and mulatos, about the cruelties of the social system, about the way someone at the bottom perceived events as they unfolded, is rare and priceless as history. In this context, her little errors and inaccuracies mean nothing.

The prose of Carolina's memoirs itself is powerful and moving, at times lyrical, often humorous, always engaging. It has been criticized for its lack of sophistication due in part to Carolina's use of nonstandard grammar and sometimes unexpected vocabulary. In this translation, we have sought to convey the texture of Carolina's Portuguese prose as clearly as possible in English. Carolina often mixes present- and past-tense verbs, and these have been preserved in English. Uncommon vocabulary that she probably integrated from her extensive reading, especially of newspapers, has been matched as nearly as possible in English—*stentorian* for *estentoria,* for example—even when a more common English word was available. In addition, the French phrases Carolina occasionally uses have been left in French.

During Carolina's childhood, the basic unit of Brazil's currency was the mil-réis, literally, a thousand réis (réis is the plural for the monetary unit real). However, Brazil's currency changed drastically from the 1920s through the Depression years through wartime and finally through the years of runaway inflation after 1950. Since Carolina wrote *Diário de Bitita* at the end of her life, during the middle 1970s, she often missed the mark in remembering how much something cost during the years in which she was growing up. The exact amounts are less important than the fact that money was such a scarce commodity in her life that she probably dwells on it in her memoirs more than would a person growing up in comfort. Her insistence, then, on relating what things cost is a reflection of how stressful her life was, never knowing from day to day whether she would have enough.

Robert M. Levine

Bitita's Diary

1

Childhood

The poor lived on a plot of state land, named the "Heritage."

There was no running water. Even with the well, they had to walk to transport the water. We lived on land that Grandpa bought from a man known as the "teacher," who owned a private school. The price of the land was fifty thousand réis.[1] Grandpa said that he did not want to die and leave his children homeless.

Our little home had a thatch roof. The walls were made of adobe covered with straw. Every year we had to change the straw, because it would rot and had to be changed before the rains came. My mother paid ten thousand réis for a cartload of straw. The floor was not made of wood, it was earth, made hard over time by many steps.

I was making my *avant-première*[2] in the world. I knew my brother's father, and I didn't know my own. Does every child have to have a father? My mother's father was Benedito José da Silva, his last name was the master's. He was a tall, peaceful black man, resigned to his

---

1. The réis is an old Brazilian monetary unit which was replaced by the cruzeiro in 1942. One conto de réis was equal to U.S.$107 in 1930, so that fifty thousand réis, the price Carolina says her grandfather paid for the house, would have been $5,350 in 1930 U.S. dollars. She was probably wrong because this price would have been too high for someone as poor as her grandfather.

2. *Avant-première*, premiere, as in the premiere of a play. Carolina uses the French.

fate as a pawn of slavery. He did not know how to read, but he spoke with a soft, pleasant voice. He was the most handsome black man I have ever seen in my life.

I thought it was so beautiful to hear my mother say, "Papa!" and my Grandpa's response, "What is it, my dear?" I envied my mother because she knew both her father and mother.

I often thought about asking her who my father was, but I didn't have the nerve. I thought it was disrespectful to ask such a question. To me, the most important people were my mother and my grandfather.

I heard the old women say that children must obey and respect their parents. One day, I heard from my mother that my father was from Araxá and that his name was João Cândido Veloso. My grandmother's name was Joana Veloso. My father played the guitar, and he didn't like to work. He only had one pair of clothes, when my mother washed his clothes, he would lay down naked. He waited for his clothes to dry to get dressed and go out. I came to the conclusion that we never have to ask anyone anything. With time we will come to know all.

Whenever my mother talked, I would get close so I could listen to her. One day, she scolded me and said, "I don't like you!" I answered her, "I'm only in this world because of you. If you hadn't been with my father I wouldn't be here." She smiled and said, "What an intelligent girl! And she's only four!" My aunt Claudimira said, "She's rude!" My mother defended me, saying that what I said was true. "She needs to be spanked. You don't know how to raise children." They started to argue and I thought, "My mother was the one who was insulted, but she isn't hurt." I realized my mother was the more intelligent one.

"Spank her! Spank the little black girl! She's only four, but as the twig is bent, so grows the tree."

"People are born what they are, they don't change!" answered my mother.

I became worried, thinking. What can "four" mean? Can it be a sickness? Can it be a treat? I went running off when I heard my brother's voice calling me to pick *garibolas*.[3]

Saturdays really worried me. What excitement! Men and women were getting ready to go to the dance. Can a dance be essential to people's lives? I asked my mother to take me to the dance. I wanted to see what a dance was, to see what caused such excitement among the

---

3. *Garibolas* are a regional fruit.

blacks. They talked about the dance over a hundred times a day . . .

A dance . . . It must be something really good, because people who talked about it always smiled. But the dance was at night, and at night I was sleepy.

I envied the women. I wanted to grow up and get a boyfriend. One day, I saw two women fighting over a man. They said, "He's mine, tramp! Bitch! Slut! If I find out you slept with him, I'll kill you!" I was shocked. Can a man be such a good thing? Why should women fight over them? So, men are better than coconut candy, peanut brittle, french fries with a steak? Why should women want to get married? Can a man be better than fried bananas with cinnamon and sugar? Can a man be tastier than rice with beans and chicken? Will I get a man when I grow up? I want a very handsome man!

My ideas changed from minute to minute, just like the clouds in the sky that make beautiful scenes. After all, if the sky were always clear blue, it wouldn't be so lovely.

One day I asked my mother, "Mama, am I a person or an animal?"

"You're a person, dear!"

"What does it mean, to be a person?"

My mother didn't answer. At night, I looked at the sky. I watched the stars and wondered, "Can it be that stars talk?" "Do they dance on Saturdays? On Saturday I will look to see if they are dancing. In the sky there must be women-stars and men-stars. Can it be that the women-stars fight over the men-stars? Can the sky be only where I am looking?"

When I went with my mother to get firewood, I saw the same sky.

In the woods, I saw a man cut down a tree. I was envious and I decided to be a man so I could be strong. I looked for my mother and begged her, "Mama, I wanna be a man. I don't like being a woman! Come on, Mama! Change me into a man!" When I wanted something, I could cry for hours and hours.

"Go to bed. Tomorrow, when you wake up, you will be a man."

"How great! How great!" I exclaimed, smiling.

When I become a man, I will buy an ax and chop down a tree. Smiling and bursting with happiness, I imagined I would need to buy a razor to shave and a rope to tie up my pants. I'd buy a horse, spurs, a broad-brimmed hat, and a whip. I intended to be an upright man. I wasn't going to drink *pinga*.[4] I wouldn't steal, because I don't like thieves.

---

4. A strong alcoholic drink made of fermented sugar cane.

I lay down and went to sleep. When I woke up, I went looking for my mother and cried, "I didn't turn into man! You fooled me!" I raised my dress so she could see I was still a girl. I followed her around, crying and begging, "I wanna be a man! I wanna be a man! I wanna be a man!" I kept it up all day long. The neighbors got impatient, "Dona[5] Cota, spank this little black girl! What a pain this girl is! What a monkey!" But my mother indulged me and said, "When you see a rainbow, you run under it. Then you will become a man."

"I don't know what a rainbow is, Mama!"

"A rainbow is an *arco-da-velha*."[6]

"Oh!"

And my gaze turned to the sky. That being the case, I would have to wait until it rained, and then the rainbow would appear. I quit crying for a few days. One night, it rained. I got up to see if I could find the rainbow. My mother came to see what I was doing. Seeing me look at the sky, she asked, "What are you looking for?"

"The rainbow, Mama."

"Rainbows don't come out at night."

My mother didn't talk much.

"Why do you want to be a man?"

"I wanna be as strong as a man. A man can chop down a tree with an ax. I wanna have a man's courage. He walks in the woods and isn't afraid of snakes. A working man makes more money than a woman, and gets rich and can buy a beautiful house to live in."

My mother smiled and took me back to bed. But when she got tired of my questions, she would beat me.

My baptismal godmother[7] defended me. She was white. When she bought a dress for herself, she would buy another for me. She combed my hair and kissed me. I thought I was important because my godmother was white.

---

5. *Dona* is a term of respect roughly equivalent to "ma'am."

6. According to the *Novo Dicionário Aurélio da Lingua Portuguesa,* 2nd edition, an *arco-da-velha* is a colloquial term for rainbow. There is a Brazilian saying, "Ela fez coisas do arco-da-velha," meaning "She did extraordinary things." Thus, one can relate the arc of the rainbow with extraordinary occurrences.

7. In Brazilian culture, the godparent relationship is an important one. People chose different godparents for the various events in their lives: baptism, first communion, marriage. The popular terms *compadre,* for men, and *comadre,* for women, designate the relationship between the child's godparents and parents.

I only wanted to eat delicious things. I remember that when I ate fried bananas with cinnamon, I said, "How tasty!" And for several days, I thought of nothing but fried bananas with cinnamon. If only I could eat a little bit more! If only I could eat that again!

I ate canned coconut candy. Oh, how delicious! And I could only think about canned coconut candy. The first time that I saw canned sardines and ate them with bread . . . Poor Mama! I didn't give her a break. I kept asking her, "I want that tasty thing! I want that tasty thing!" And I followed my mother all around.

My aunt Teresa asked, "What does she want?"

I heard my mother say, "She wants sardines with bread."

And that's how I learned that those tasty things were sardines.

I was unbearable. When I wanted something, I cried night and day until I got it. I was very persistent in all of my whims. I thought the most important thing was to get what you wanted. And my wishes were satisfied. The only way my mother could live in peace was to give in to me. She was tolerant. She looked at me, smiled, and said, "Look at her face!" She didn't beat me.

The neighbors looked at me and said, "What an ugly little black girl! She's not only ugly, she's nasty! If I were her mother, I would have killed her already!" My mother looked at me and said, "A mother doesn't kill her child. What a mother needs is lots of patience! Mr. Eurípedes Barsanulfo told me she was a poet!"

2

The Godmothers

When my mother went to work, she left me with my godmother, Siá[1] Maruca. When I turned seven, my mother invited Dona Matilde to be my confirmation sponsor.[2] She bought me a chintz dress to wear. When I put the dress on, I thought I was very beautiful. I looked at everyone who passed me on the street to see if they were looking at me because I was wearing a new dress. How good it is to be a child, when everything new has tremendous value for us! I was barefoot because my mother couldn't buy a pair of "angel-feet"[3] shoes for me.

I went to the church with my godmother. She rented a carriage. The driver was my mother's mulatto cousin, José Marcelino. He charged us five hundred réis per person. My godmother gave him ten thousand réis. "Wow! She has a lot of money! I am important now, I have a rich godmother!" Grown-ups walked through the

---

1. A shortened form of *sinhá*, which, in turn, is a corruption of the word *senhora*, mistress, formerly used by black slaves to address the white mistresses. Carolina later tells us that Siá Maruca lives with her grandfather, but they are not married until just before her grandfather dies.

2. In Brazil, the confirmation sponsor would be called a confirmation godmother.

3. In the Portuguese, *"pé de anjo."* This probably refers to a type of shoe that was in style when Carolina was a child.

streets with the children, holding their hands. The church was packed. The altars were decorated with pink flowers.

My godmother genuflected. I asked her, "Why did you kneel, ma'am?"

"Whenever we are in church, we have to kneel to greet the Holy Sacrament on the altar." The rural women were in town to confirm their children. They wore long print dresses. They had their hair put up in buns or curly or braided with ribbons. The bishop was from Uberaba. My godmother explained to me that the priest would baptize the children, and the bishop would confirm them.

The candles were lit. Those who entered the church carried flowers, and the combination of the colors made the holy temple cheerful. The scents of the incense and flowers blended, and that, for me, was dazzling.

After the confirmation, my godmother and I walked home. I found a handkerchief, and my godmother said I could use it after I washed it.

I thought, "Now I have to obey my rich godmother, who has ten thousand réis." I also thought, "I have three godmothers, who is the best one? One is black, the other is mulatta, and another is white." The white one was so nice that I nicknamed her the sweet godmother. Siá Maruca was black, but she was loving, she combed and braided my hair. Godmother Matilde, who confirmed me, was mulatta. Godmother Mariinha was the white one. My mother always said, "When the mother dies, it's the godmothers' obligation to raise her godchild, a godmother is a second mother. You can't curse your godmothers, you have to respect them."

I was skinny and the new dress was loose, I looked like a toothpick in it. On our way home, I paid attention to everything. What joy when we got to my godmother's house! We had lunch at the table. Rice, beans, cracklings, pork, and okra. The dessert: rice pudding with cinnamon. What a treat! I shouted enthusiastically, "If I only could have this again!" Then I was ashamed. My mother had told me to be well-behaved with my godmothers. If a mother were to send her child to hell, only the godmother could save her godchild.

For me, life consisted of eating, growing, and playing. I thought, "The world is a good place to live in. I'm never going to die, so I won't have to leave the world. The world will always be mine! If I die, I will never see the sun, the moon, or the stars again. If I were to meet God, I'd ask him, 'God, will you give me the world?' "

I spent that day with my godmother. At eight thirty at night I went home, but my wish was to live with my godmother forever. I didn't tell anyone what a wonderful day I had had, but I couldn't stop thinking about my godmother.

I went to bed and soon fell asleep. When the birds started their morning symphony, I got out of bed, washed, and ran over to my godmother's house. When she opened the door I jumped inside and asked, "Bless me, godmother!"[4] She was surprised and answered, "God . . . b . . . bless you."

I spent the day with my godmother. She gave me fried bananas with cinnamon. "Yum, it's so tasty!" I was very happy with that godmother who gave me delicious things to eat. Wow, it is so nice to have a godmother!

The following day I got up and ran over to her house. As she opened the door, I said, "Bless me, godmother." She answered, "God . . . b . . . bless you." I spent the day with my godmother, but I didn't eat any sweets. That afternoon, I returned home disappointed. But even so, when the next day broke, I ran over there. When she opened the door, there I was, "Bless me, godmother!"

She didn't answer me, but murmured, "Hum, hum, hum." She looked at me and said, "If only I knew, I would have never confirmed this girl!" I was so hurt. I went back home dejected. And I swore "I will never again go back to my godmother's house." In the beginning, she wasn't concerned. Months and years passed. From time to time, she sent us a dish of cooked beef. Just the smell of it made my mouth water! We ate it. I ate most of it, because she was sending it to me. My brother envied me, "You certainly have a good godmother!" My mother wanted me to take the dishes back. I didn't go, so I wouldn't break my vow. So, my brother returned them.

She was raising a servant girl who did basic housework: going out in the morning to get meat scraps for the pigs.

My godmother got sick, I didn't go visit her. She died, I didn't go to the funeral. I didn't go see her for the last time. I was obstinate and said that when I cut myself off from someone, it's for good. They prayed the rosary. I didn't join them.

My godfather Cassiano and the servant girl took care of the house. In the morning, the girl went off to the hotel to get leftover meat. She

---

4. Asking a godparent, parent, or other older person for a blessing is a Brazilian tradition. It is a sign of affection, respect, and submission to their authority.

separated the fat, saving the little pieces of meat. Then, she boiled water and poured it over the scraps.

My godfather was at home. He had left work until he got his life back on track. He watched the girl work to see if she knew how to take care of the house. She took a storage can, removed the congealed fat from the scraps and said, "Alright, Uncle Cassiano, you can feed the pigs with these scraps because I've already saved the fat."

Worried, my godfather asked, "What do you do with that fat?"

"I'm gonna cook with it. Godmother always cooked that way."

"And the meat you saved?"

"Godmother cut off the meat, then she chopped it in little pieces and stewed it with green onions and tomatoes and made *angu* stew."[5]

"What about that stale bread you saved?"

"Godmother softened that stale bread with goat's milk and put it in the oven. We ate it with coffee, and it was good."

"What about all the money I gave her for grocery shopping?"

"She saved it in a can."

"Where's the can?"

The girl led my godfather to the bedroom, pulled out a chest that was under the bed, took out a sack that was in the chest, and in the sack was a can with the money.

My godfather was surprised by the number of two thousand réis coins; five, ten, fifty, one hundred and two hundred thousand réis bills. They spent the afternoon counting the money: thirteen contos! He mulled over what she could have been saving that money for. He asked.

"She said that it was to build a home with a porch she could walk back and forth on."

"Bitch! Trash! Giving me leftovers to eat, just to save money! She must've been nuts! Did she eat it too?"

"She ate it, godfather."

My godfather gave a long sigh, commenting, "Unfortunately, a man doesn't know his wife very well, he never realizes who he's marrying. How long have I been eating this food? Such a tremendous sacrifice for a house with a porch just to walk back and forth on."

When my mother found out, she spit and said, "She used to invite me to eat her *angu* stew. I always promised I would go, but I never had the time."

---

5. A popular Brazilian stew made with corn flour, milk and occasionally meat.

My brother remarked, "What doesn't kill us, makes us stronger."

With the thirteen contos, my godfather bought some land to plant. Fifteen *alqueires*[6] of land. It was his dream come true, but he relished it in silence. He always said that land was the best investment. People who buy land aren't getting poorer, they're getting richer. He remarried. I heard he got rich.

As you can see, everyone has a dream that feeds the soul. My godmother could have built her house with a porch to walk back and forth on . . .

When my godmother Matilde had nothing in the house to eat, she would take an empty plate and a fork and stand in the front door of her house, pretending she was eating, and saying, "I do that so my neighbors will see that I don't go hungry, because there's always a neighbor with a big mouth."

---

6. A land measurement unit. One *alqueire* was the equivalent of 4 *hectares* or 84 acres.

3

The Holiday

I was horrified when I saw women hugging men. I thought, "Why is it that women hug men and that men are so happy with the caresses of women?"

What worried my mother was my state of mind. If someone asked her "Is your daughter crazy?" She answered, "She seems crazy, but she isn't."

I remember when my mother had a baby girl. She was born dead and rotten, with her flesh falling off her bones. The people who came to visit her left vomiting and remarking, "I never saw anyone born like that." They said it was syphilis. I thought, "What could syphilis be? When will I learn all that there is in the world?" My mother said that she worked too hard, washing woven cotton and wool blankets. When wet, they weighed seventy kilos.

Sometimes I noticed the excitement of the people buying cloth to make clothing to wear on New Year's Day. Why is it that they all talked and smiled on this day? And these days were celebrated with dances. Who could have invented dances? But I noticed that New Year's Day was a day just like the others, with its miseries and afflictions.

After the New Year was *carnaval*.[1] So, the world is always like this? Every year it's the same thing? My mother said no.

The only month that I knew about was the month of May. And the blacks went out begging. They went out with a flag bearing the portrait of Saint Benedict.[2] When they got to the rich people's houses, the ladies waved the flag in the bedrooms and livingrooms, asking the saint to help them. Even though they had houses to live in and to rent out, beautiful clothes, abundant food, cars, bathrooms with hot water to bathe every day. Living in comfort, they still asked for help from the saints. Wow! Could it be that the rich aren't happy with what they have? Why all this nonsense to get rich if, when you die, you leave it all behind! They gave alms, but made innumerable petitions.

On the day of the holiday, Américo de Sousa, the son of a rich man, was happy and playful. To scare the blacks who danced the *congada*[3] in the streets, he got up at three o'clock in the morning and made three crosses of ashes in the middle of the bridge that went to Rosário Plaza. When the blacks who were dancing the *congada* were going to cross the bridge and saw the crosses, they got afraid, thinking it was black magic. Ameriquinho,[4] together with the other whites, laughed.

But José Santana, who was the toast of the party and had a *congada* suit, jumped over the ashen crosses and was named a hero by the people. After Santana had jumped over the crosses, the spell should be broken for him.

What I noticed is that whites never went to black people's parties. One day a man who had no legs showed up. He passed out some

---

1. *Carnaval* is the Brazilian celebration of Mardi Gras, or Shrove Tuesday, which takes place during the three days immediately preceding Ash Wednesday and Lent, the forty-day period that Roman Catholics dedicate to fasting, repentance, and atonement. A traditional part of the *carnaval* celebration is dressing up in costumes and wearing elaborate make-up. Although in popular practice in Brazil today the parties may begin earlier, the traditional celebration of carnaval takes place during the three days prior to Ash Wednesday, as indicated here. See the *Novo Dicionário Aurélio da Língua Portuguesa,* 2nd ed.

2. Saint Benedict was a sixteenth-century Italian saint called the "Black" or the "Moor." According to *The Book of Saints* (New York: Macmillan, 1944), he was born in 1526 of parents of African descent in a village near Messina in Sicily. His parents were slaves, but he was made a freeman. In Brazil, he was known as protector of the slaves and, in popular culture, his figure is associated with the *congadas.*

3. The *congada* is a pantomimic folk dance of African origin.

4. Ameriquinho is the diminutive of Américo.

invitations, inviting the people to go hear him play the guitar at the Recreio movie theater. He played the waltz "Saudades do Matão."[5] The waltz was already old hat. It was not a success. I think he was just learning, because he didn't know how to meld the melody he played with the music he sang. Or else he was a liar. They booed the poor man! "Get out! Hit the road!" What laughter. They all smiled, except me.

Because the sadness I noticed in the artist's face revealed that there must be something very sad in his life. Could he have a complex because he didn't have any legs?

There were times when I was so afraid of the world! It was when I heard men talking about how hard it was for a man to find work. The world isn't a paradise for man. The war with Paraguay[6] was tragic, men killed each other with cannons and bombs of dynamite.

When I was with adults, I heard say about things I didn't understand. When I was with children, we played ring-around-the-rosie, we told fairy tales. And about the princess who went to dance in hell because she was the devil's lover.

The people were excited about the June holidays.[7] And they all talked about Saint Anthony, Saint John the Baptist, and Saint Peter.

A woman had made a king cut off Saint John the Baptist's head! I thought, "Women also have power in the world! Ah! then I am also going to have power, only I'm not going to permit them to cut off men's heads. Women fight over men, they like to kiss them, they cry because they love men, and then they have a man's head cut off."

How I hated the woman who had Saint John the Baptist's head cut off. I didn't sleep, thinking about the pain he had felt. It was King Herod who had it cut off. Wow! So kings are powerful. I got afraid of

---

5. The name of the song means something like "Longings for the Countryside."

6. In 1865, the Triple Alliance—Brazil, Argentina, and Uruguay—was allied in a war against Paraguay. Paraguay was defeated in 1870.

7. The *Festas Juninas,* or June holidays, are the feast days of Saint Anthony, Saint John the Baptist, and Saint Peter. According to Luís da Câmara Cascudo's *Dicionário do Folclore Brasileiro* (São Paulo: Melhoramentos, 1979), Saint Anthony, one of the most popular saints in Brazil, is celebrated on June 13. Traditionally, he is the protector of marriages and he is known as a powerful matchmaker for young women who wish to marry. Saint John, Jesus Christ's cousin, is honored on June 24. In Brazil, he is celebrated with bonfires and dances. Saint Peter is honored on June 29, together with Saint Paul.

kings, thank God that here in Brazil we don't have a king. A king shouldn't be bad. He should be good.

I heard that they had crucified Jesus Christ. That Jesus Christ was also a king, but more powerful than the other kings.

The children were happy because on Saint John's Day, they were going to eat sweet potatoes and drink *quentão*.[8] The men cut firewood to make the bonfires, and prepared the canopies for the dance.

Saint John's Day and Saint Anthony's Day were favored for weddings. Women said, "I got married on Saint Anthony's Day so he would protect me." But I heard that it's the man who should protect the woman after they get married. How beautiful a child's mind was!

I found the world ugly and sad when I was hungry. After I ate lunch, I found the world beautiful. I asked my mother "The world is so good! Is it always like this?" She didn't answer me, she just gave me such a sad look, a look that worried me. But I insisted, "Mama! Mama ... tell me about the world. What does 'world' mean?" She gave me two slaps, and I ran out crying. My aunt Claudimira said, "You have to do something with this little black girl. She's going to make you crazy."

---

8. *Quentão* is hot sugar-cane rum mixed with sugar, cinnamon, and ginger.

4

Being Poor

My mother spanked me every day. When I didn't get a beating, I missed it. Then I understood that Grandpa was my protector.

My brother was the favorite.

When my mother beat me, I went to my grandfather's house. It was a shack with a sloping roof, covered with thatch. Similar to the Indian huts I saw in books. Grandpa's house was so poor!

He got four pitchforks and buried them in the ground. He put up two beams and the roof planks. There was a bed with a mattress made from a burlap sack full of straw. A woven blanket, a wooden mortar, a spinning wheel, a wooden bowl for washing feet, and two iron pans. They didn't have any plates, they ate from wooden bowls.

Siá Maruca, my grandfather's wife, was very good. She didn't complain about life. She was cheerful. I don't know if that smile was a laugh of resignation.

Every afternoon, Grandpa prayed the rosary. We knelt in front of the crucifix. I was horrified to see the nails in Christ's hands. What pain he must have felt!

A man would have to be very perverse to dare to drive those nails into Jesus Christ's hands. There is no glory for those who kill their fellow man. They aren't going to get any trophies.

Grandpa was already complaining that he was feeling pain in his kidneys, but nonetheless he went to hear Mr. Manoel Nogueira. He told us that the farmers were desperate, the Italians were leaving the farms. When they saw that the white farmhands were no longer interested in the harsh labor of the country, they went to the cities in search of farmhands. Color didn't matter to them. They didn't quibble. How many promises! They told the blacks, "You can go to my farm. I had a dance hall built for you. I'm going to send for the accordionist, Juritão Marangoni, to play so you can dance. And, at the end of the year, I'll bring the jazz band Bico Doce from Ribeirão Preto to play for you." But the blacks didn't go because there was work in the city, too, they didn't get very far.

And Mr. Nogueira said, "They took Saint Benedict out of the fields and put up Saint Januarius.[1] It's a quirk of Brazilians, they have the cure in their own country, but they prefer a European import."

And the coffee harvests got weaker. The last resort was that the farmers left their lands and established themselves in the city. Many left their lands crying, "It's the beginning of the end of Brazil because now we're going to the city and we're going to be consumers, it will be a minority that will produce for a majority to consume." And they promised the blacks, "Go back to the fields because we're going to treat you well. We accept your demands." The majority of blacks were illiterate. They had already lost faith in the ruling class and in themselves.

The slave trade began in the year 1515. It ended in the year 1888. The blacks were enslaved for almost 400 years.

When a black man got old, he would go out begging. He begged in the country. Only those who were licensed beggars could beg in the city. The town council issued a metal tag with a number after the person was examined by a doctor and his handicap was proven. And the beggar couldn't lend money and charge interest. They were inspected.

My mother washed clothes each day and earned five thousand réis. She brought me with her. I sat under the trees. My gaze kept straying through the windows, watching the rich people eating at the table. And envious of the blacks who could work in the rich people's houses.

One day, my mother was washing clothes. She intended to wash

---

1. This is probably Saint Januarius, the patron saint of Naples, San Gennaro in Italian. According to *The Book of Saints,* he was martyred by beheading in 304 and his body was buried in the church of Naples.

them quickly to get money and buy us food. The police arrested her.

I got nervous. But I couldn't say anything. If I protested, the soldier would hit me with a rubber whip.

And the news spread, "Cota was arrested."

"Why?"

When my brother found out that my mother was in jail, he began to cry. We walked all around the jail, crying. At midnight, they decided to release her. We were happy. She thanked us, then cried. I thought, "It's only black women who are arrested."

When Mr. Manoel Nogueira found out, he was distressed, "Poor Cota. She never hurts anyone."

In order to arrest someone, there has to be a reason. What I can't understand is how they could hire an illiterate guy to be a policeman. Of two hundred men, only ten knew how to read. Hiring an illiterate policeman was the last resort. When they got paid, they made an X to prove they had received their salary.

One day, I was walking down the street, I was happy. I'd gotten a sweet lime that I was going to offer to my mother when Humbertinho appeared and took the lime away from me. I cried. He was white. He had served in the army. Sometimes he wore his uniform. He looked like Rudolph Valentino,[2] he was more handsome. When I found him, I cursed, "Give me my lime! Give me my lime." Everyone was afraid of him, he was the judge's son. And the judge has people arrested. He found an outlet for his satanic instinct.

One afternoon, when I was passing in front of his house, he accosted me and threw several limes at my face, my legs. What pain! Then I cursed, "Common dog, no one around here likes you! Go away, you're a dirty guy."

They went to tell Doutor[3] Brand who went to see our argument. He didn't understand why those limes were scattered on the ground. I cursed, "This wretch is always grabbing the breasts of poor girls, he squeezes, and leaves them crying, but you're not going to lay a hand on me."

Doutor Brand interfered, "Don't you have any manners?"

"I do, it's your son who doesn't have any."

---

2. Rudolph Valentino, the silent movie star, came to represent the epitome of a handsome male lead.

3. Traditionally, any person who holds a bachelor's degree in Brazil is called *doutor*, literally, doctor. It is a mark of social as well as economic distinction.

"Shut up. I can have you put away."

"So that your son can do filthy things to me, like he does with all the girls that you pick up? It's better to go to hell than to your house. Doutor Brand, here everyone talks about you, but no one has the nerve to talk to you. Grown-ups don't have the nerve to come up and speak! Your son goes into the poor people's yards and steals fruit."

They went to tell my mother that I was fighting with Doutor Brand. They went to tell the military police.[4] The people ran to see the fight. When Doutor Brand walked in my direction, I didn't run and he didn't hit me. My mother pulled at me, "Shut up, bitch!"

I shouted, "Leave me alone, this is a man to man fight." I said, "Look Doutor Brand, your son stole a lime from me. Everyone is afraid of him, but I'm not! He isn't invited to rich people's parties because the rich don't want to have anything to do with him."

"Shut up, you insolent little nigger."

"Your son is the insolent one because he's the judge's son, he doesn't respect anyone."

When he was going to hit me, I told him, "Rui Barbosa[5] said that whites shouldn't steal, they shouldn't kill. They shouldn't take advantage because it's the white man who is in control. The key to the world is in white people's hands, the white man has to be superior to give an example. The white man has to be like the conductor of an orchestra. The white man has to toe the line."

Doutor Brand said, "Let's stop, I'm going to leave your city."

My mother took my hand and took me home. The people begged, "Don' beat her." Even the military policemen didn't mess with me. My mother didn't let me go out of the house. Three days later, Doutor Brand left the city. He said he was going to Rio de Janeiro.

How sorry I felt for Doutor Brand. I cried in pity for Dona Sinhá, the judge's wife. What a good woman!

---

4. In Brazil, there is a military police force and a civil police force. The military police force derived from the old National Guard, the emperor's personal army. With the formation of the Republic, the National Guard turned into a military police force. Carolina uses the term *soldado*, translated throughout as "military policeman," to refer to a member of this military police force, and the term *policial*, translated throughout as "policeman," to refer to a member of the civil police force. Both the military and the civil police have authority over civilians.

5. Rui Barbosa (1849–1923) was a Brazilian journalist and politician who supported the Republican movement and opposed slavery.

When they saw me in the streets, the people smiled at me, saying, "What an intelligent girl, she defended us! She cleaned up the city." Everyone gave me presents. I got new and used dresses. The daughters of the pharmacist, José Neto, gave me two embroidered cotton dresses and asked me, "Do you know how to read?"

"No, ma'am."

"Wow, when you do know . . . well then! You have promise, girl."

They said that it was Rui Barbosa's words that I quoted that stopped the judge. That I spoke through the intervention of a spirit. It's that I heard Mr. Nogueira read *O Estado de São Paulo.*[6]

Our life improved a little bit when my mother went to work for Dona Mariquinha, José Saturnino's wife. What a good family! Cultured people. They were Spiritualists. Their yard was large, with several fruit trees.

I went with the boss's son who was going to kill birds. The birds already knew us. They flew away when they saw us. Ebantho and I became friends. A delightful friendship, just playing together.

In Mr. José Saturnino's boarding house there lived a blind man, Mr. Epifânio Rodrigues, who was a beggar.

When the children guided him along the streets, they stole his money. What nerve to steal from a blind man! A thief can't go to heaven. When I led him, I turned over all the money to him.

He used to say, "Oh! Bitita! You are so upright that you should have been born a man. An honest and upright man is the sun on earth." I thought that I should go under the rainbow so I would turn into an upright man in order to help mankind. And I cried when he commented, "How sad it is to be blind. Oh! God! why did you give me this hardship! What did I do wrong to receive such a tremendous punishment. The evils that bad men practice sicken me mentally. There are those who, when they have sight, use it to practice evil. There are those who spend the night studying, working hard to invent a powerful weapon to annihilate humanity."

I was sorry for him. If I could only give him one of my eyes! But I can't! I became enraged thinking that all people should be equal. I repeated Mr. Epifânio's words in my head, "What wrong did I do to God to receive such a tremendous punishment!"

So, the God that the black man says is our Father can punish a man

---

6. *The State of São Paulo,* an important newspaper with national circulation.

in such a merciless way! What a harsh punishment! What should I do to avoid punishments from God?

I heard about Saint Luiza who was the protector of the blind. I begged her to give new eyes to the three blind men in my city. They were Mr. Epifânio, Blind João, who was black, and blind Mr. José. He was a faith healer. He blessed children who were sick because of the evil eye, and women who had headaches. He blessed them like this:

As God was, God is.
God does whatever He wills.
My good Jesus of Nazareth
Our Lord blessed His son so He would cry.
I bless in the name of Mary in order to cure
Beautiful Star, Precious Maiden,
Take away the illnesses
from the body of this Christian. Amen!

My mind recorded everything I heard, effortlessly.

He died drunk. His was the most beautiful corpse I ever saw. What a pity. Such a good man. The world must be horrible for a blind man. I heard a woman say that the body is the envelope of the soul.

Blind João played the guitar and sang. All of the young black women would seek him out to bring him to the dances. He was almost a sultan in that setting, hearing his name called by several tones of voice: João! João! João.

But, when he wanted to get married, he didn't find a woman. He became sad and got sick. He didn't go to the doctor. He died at twenty-three.

This is why he was blind. He was four years old. His mother, Dona Joaquina, gave him a dish of very hot soup. Immediately afterward, she gave him a cold bath. He caught a cold that got into his eyes. If João had found a woman, perhaps he would have had the strength to tolerate his odyssey and fight in life.

Poor women didn't have any free time to care for their homes. At six in the morning, they had to be in their mistresses' houses to light the fire and prepare the morning meal. What a horrible thing! Those who had mothers, left their children and their homes with them.

The maids had to cook, clean, and iron. The meals had to be prepared with a lot of fuss: little tomato baskets stuffed with mayonnaise, little potato baskets stuffed with ground ham, olives, etc. The meals were served like this: first, a soup; after the soup, rice, beans, meat, and salad were served. When they served fish, other plates and silverware were used. Finally, dessert and coffee.

How many dishes and silverware and pans to be washed! And the silverware had to be polished. Wash the floor tiles and dry them with cloths. They left work at eleven at night. They worked exclusively in the kitchen. It was common to hear black women say, "My God! I'm so tired!"

They were allowed to bring the leftover food home. And in their homes, their children, whom they called the little black ones, stayed awake waiting for mama to arrive with the delicious food from the rich houses. At dinner, the cooks made extra food, to be leftover. The food that the employers ate at lunch, they didn't eat at dinner.

A good cook earned thirty thousand réis a month. When the month ended and the cook got paid, she felt like a heroine. She praised herself saying, "I'm strong! Not just any woman could stand to cook for Doutor Souza."

What pride, what vanity, to be the cook of Doutor José da Cunha or of President Franklin Vieira and José Alfonso. It was common to hear the rich say, "Do you know who you're talking to? I'm a big shot!" And the pretentious black women sometimes said, "You know who you're talkin' to? I'm the president's cook."

On Saturdays, the cooks went to dances. What torture to cook on Sundays, sleepily. But after lunch, they could go out, have fun until four o'clock, and return to prepare dinner. And they never got enough.

On the following Saturday, they again went dancing until six in the morning. On Sundays, they had to go to work at seven because the mistresses wanted to sleep until seven.

When the cooks felt sleepy, they washed their faces in cold water to wake themselves up. The only fear was of over-salting the food and the mistress calling them to account. There were many people to work and very few openings. The mistress was treated as if she were a saint on the altar. If the mistresses were nervous, the maids had to say, "Yes, ma'am!" If they were friendly, they had to say, "Yes, ma'am!" A poor man must always be conceived, born, grow, and live with patience in order to tolerate the egotism of the masters of the world. Because only rich men could say, "Do you know who you're talking to?" to show their superiority.

If the boss's son slapped the cook's son, she couldn't complain in order not to lose her job. But if the cook had a daughter, poor little black girl! The boss's son would use her for his sexual initiation. Girls who were still thinking about dolls, about children's songs and dances, were brutalized by the sons of Mr. Pereira, Moreira, Oliveira, and other filth who came from overseas.

After nine months, the little black girl was the mother of a mulatto or a brown baby. And the people kept attributing its paternity, "It must be this guy's child! It must be that guy's child!" But the mother, black, ignorant, and unschooled, couldn't reveal that her baby was the grandson of Doutor X or Y. Because the mother would lose her job. What a struggle for that mother to raise that child! How many single mothers committed suicide, others died consumptive from crying so much.

The black father was voiceless; if he tried to complain, the boss silenced him, "Shut up, lazy nigger! Bum!"

The only refuge was to give oneself over to God, who is the advocate of the poor. And if Doutor Oliveira who studied in Coimbra[7] were to say, "Black thief . . ." that would pass from mouth to mouth. And that black man, without ever having stolen anything, was a thief. Because the *doutor* who had studied in Coimbra said so! And he would never be rehabilitated. And the black man was regional, he didn't have the nerve to leave his native land. He stayed right there and became the butt of the young boys' jokes.

And Mr. Oliveira's son, after having enough of seducing young poor girls, would decide to marry Mr. Moreira's daughter, she was rich. He would court her very respectfully. When the blacks got together they would say, "There is a Bahian,[8] Doutor Rui Barbosa, who wants blacks to go to school, but the whites say that they already freed the blacks and that's enough."

But Rui said that freedom without learning and without education wouldn't benefit them. An unschooled black will be a nomad, indolent, and not capable of being integrated into society. He won't be an arm to move the nation forward. He will always be a mouth. An illiterate person doesn't have the power to evolve in life. He will always be a musician who plays by ear.

7. A city in Portugal that is the location of a famous, old university, the University of Coimbra. It was common for the Brazilian elite to study in Coimbra.
8. A person from the state of Bahia, in the northeast of Brazil.

And the blacks liked Rui, and Princess Isabel.[9] My grandfather used to tell that, after the slaves were freed, when a black girl was born, when she was baptized, the priest said without even asking her name: Isabel.

Rui said that the black man should remain working in agriculture. That a country needs to have an agricultural class. He could stay at work until three in the afternoon, and study at night. But the *doutores* from Coimbra said that it was the children of the ruling class who should study, and not those who should be ruled, that the master and the servant could not have equal wisdom. Rui said that wisdom is natural, study is for informing. He died in the year 1923. What a loss for the country! Both his friends and enemies exclaimed, "Is it possible that we're going to have a government that will prepare a Brazil for Brazilians?"

---

9. Princess Isabel de Bragança—Isabel Cristina Leopoldina Augusta Micaela Gabriela Rafaela Gonzaga (1846–1921)—the daughter of Emperor Dom Pedro II, signed a decree abolishing slavery in Brazil in 1888. This decree is known as the Emancipation Law. Most of the biographical information on figures from Brazilian history included in these notes comes from Boris Fausto's *História do Brasil* (São Paulo: EDUSP, 1996).

5

A Little History

General Isidoro Dias Lopes's revolt broke out in 1924.[1] Nobody knew the reason for that rebellion. Was it opposition to President Artur Bernardes?[2]

They promoted a campaign: "Donate gold to benefit Brazil." And even in Sacramento, my birth place, gold collectors showed up. At every home they visited, they received something made of gold. After all, the lady of that house didn't want to be shown up. They gave gold, and received an alloy and copper ring with the inscription, "I gave gold to benefit Brazil." And the rich ladies would wear those rings ostentatiously.

The word spread that they collected ninety kilos of gold. And Brazil continued with its illiterate people, hoping for a successor to Rui Barbosa. He was the trade-mark politician of that time. Even dead, he still predominated.

And I thought, "Why do these good men who like to help the people

---

1. According to E. Bradford Burns's *A History of Brazil*, 2nd edition (New York: Columbia University Press, 1980), this revolt was carried out by young army officers who were opposed to President Artur Bernardes's administration. Their leader was a retired general, Isidoro Dias Lopes (1863–1949). The revolt broke out on July 5, 1924. Further information on many of the historical facts included in these footnotes can be found in Burns's text.
2. Artur da Silva Bernardes (1875–1955) governed Brazil from 1922 to 1926.

die? The ones who really deserve to die are only the good-for-nothings." The people, talking about the revolution, said that there were many robberies in the big cities, that terrified families left their homes, and the thieves took advantage of the owners' absence.

The revolution made some people rich and others poor. And that revolution left Brazil in disorder. And on the flag is written "*Order and Progress*"!

The soldiers wore a pin in the shape of the Brazilian map. It was green with the inscription "This land has an owner!" To those of us who lived in the countryside, there came only some very adulterated rumors.

The revolution didn't affect President Artur Bernardes's administration. He used to say, "I am the Head of State. I came here to govern. I will not follow those who talk a lot. Those who have too many liberal ideas, those frustrated blowhards. I have a moral obligation to my people. Who recognize my will to serve them. I consider myself a public servant."

And the revolution was like a thunderstorm.

The people said that before his birth, Mr. Artur Bernardes had taken a course in diplomacy in his mother's womb. He defeated his opposition with his most powerful weapon: education. They could fight with him, but he didn't fight with anyone. He grew up and became a man. He wasn't one of those guys who are only men physically. But remain immature, childish.

In 1925, schools started admitting black female students. But, when the black girls came home from school, they were crying, saying they didn't want to go back to school because the whites said that the blacks smelled bad.

The teachers only accepted the black students because they were forced to. But if the black student failed, his mother would go talk to the teacher, "You didn't let my kid go on to second grade because he's black, but he already knows how to read and write his a-b-c's. Júlio Barges's kids passed and José Afonso's granddaughters did too.[3] If I could only spoil the life of a teacher like you with the evil-eye!"

The teachers didn't answer. They understood there were two differ-

---

3. Júlio Barges and José Afonso are "white" names. The use of these names implies that these children were promoted to an upper grade because they were white.

ent worlds. An educated person and an ignorant one could never reach an agreement. They said every career had its negative side. Afterward they lamented, "See what the abolitionists did! Now those people think they can talk to us as equals. I, at the time of abolition, would have sent all those repugnant people back to Africa."

And the *doutores* from Coimbra insulted Dom Pedro II, "Dog! He should have lost his citizenship, these lands should have remained a Portuguese colony."

At that time, the only two important black men were Patrício Teixeira, a singer, and Dr. Azevedo Costa, from Uberaba. And the blacks remarked, "Thank God we now have illustrious blacks, we have a black man who sings on records, and another who writes prescriptions. Pharmacies sell the medicines that he prescribes. Dr. Azevedo Costa has a hospital that he built."

I was little, and I heard the old people talking and thought, "I can't die without meeting Dr. Azevedo Costa. How could he have become a doctor? Oh! If only it were possible for me to become a doctor ... I would be Dr. Bitita."

In the city, the most respected man was Mr. Manoel Nogueira. He was a mulatto. And the mulatto is a hybrid in society. He interacts with whites and blacks. And with the last name Nogueira, he must have been the son of some *doutor* from Coimbra. Mr. Manoel Nogueira spent the day with whites, because he was a Justice officer. And in the evenings, he used to sit at the front door of his house, and read the newspaper *O Estado de São Paulo* so we could hear some excerpts from Rui Barbosa's speeches; for example, that every state should give the blacks some land to cultivate. But this project was not approved by the Chamber of Deputies.[4]

Brazil had opened the door to Italian immigration. We would receive six thousand Italians, two thousand would go to São Paulo, two thousand to Rio Grande do Sul, a thousand to Rio de Janeiro, and another thousand to the state of Minas.

They came to be tenant farmers, they would lease land from the landowners for planting. And the Brazilians had to respect them. When the Italians arrived, they saw that the only one who could help them with the hard labor was the black man.

---

4. This refers to the Federal Chamber of Deputies, part of the Brazilian legislature, similar to the House of Representatives.

The Italians who came were selected. Healthy, good teeth, and they knew how to read. A family of eight people tended fifteen thousand coffee plants. They ate meat, polenta, cheese, and soup. Their bread was home-made. The loaves were huge, they cut off slices. They were well-fed.

What a relief for the blacks! Working for the Italians, they would make one thousand réis a day. At the end of the week, what a fortune! Six thousand réis, and the blacks bought shoes and even the famous cashmere suit. For the Italians, friends were never lacking, because they were courteous and kind to the blacks.

When the Italians had dances on Saturdays, they would let their daughters dance with the black men, which made them proud. On Sundays, they met at the corner to remark, "I danced with Concheta. I danced with Pina."

On Mondays, the black man who danced with Concheta, and the black man who danced with Pina would work as if they were four men. Thrilled, because the Italians weren't arrogant.

They cultivated all the grains, raised pigs, chickens, and cows. They didn't face any opposition from the landowners. An agricultural Brazil was a rich Brazil. It was the famous Brazil. The harvests were abundant.

On weekdays, the workers disappeared. They returned to town on Saturdays. Their wives worked for rich families. A *doutor* made five hundred thousand réis a month, and lived in a palatial house. His servants were: a cook, a maid, a laundress, a chauffeur, and a seamstress. They all ate at the *doutor*'s house. And they were nicely dressed. The *doutor*'s car was a Buick. The women worked all year long, at the end of the year, if they were to balance the accounts of their earnings, they had nothing.

The law ruled. A military policeman was the authority. And there was order in the city. On Sundays, the guys ruled the city. They were allowed to sing, drink, and even fight. But, on Monday, if the police found a guy on the streets he had to have a good excuse for why he was loafing on a day meant for work. He would say, "My wife had a baby."

And if he hadn't told the truth, he would be arrested.

Brazilian coffee was famous in Europe. And the landowners who sold so much coffee were uneducated men who, when they got rich, made us call them "colonel." And it was colonel everywhere.

The Italians gradually changed from tenant farmers into landowners, they bought land in the big cities. They built houses, villas to rent them out. And they ruled the cities, and lived off the income from the rents.

The owners lived on the upper floors of the houses, and the blacks lived in the basements. When the blacks drank and made noise in the basement, the Italians stamped their feet on the floor. It was the signal asking for silence! And the voices stopped.

The Italians built bakeries, stores, and there was lots of work. Except that the workers, with no education, didn't know how to read. They didn't know how to manage the money they made. The money went to buy Sunday clothes, to stroll around the public squares in, and to be admired in at dances. They didn't like to be known for their poor wardrobe.

At dawn, they left town. They were afraid of going to jail with a military policeman at their side. What shame, everybody staring at them! If it was cold out, the black man would sweat. When he was released, he would disappear forever. But whites weren't arrested.

And these prerogatives, these immunities, these concessions made the powerful even more authoritarian. The poor man's child, from birth, was already destined to work with a hoe. The rich people's children were raised at boarding schools. It was a time when only the minority could get an education. The literate minority was shrinking.

The worst thing about this was when a doctor prescribed medication for a lay person, they made mistakes because they didn't know how to tell time. The clock was a complicated machine with numbers and little dots and that tick-tock. And they didn't know how to read the instructions.

Dr. José da Cunha was our doctor, he prescribed a laxative for Mr. "Blind" José, and a medicine to take after the laxative. Dona Ambrosina, Mr. "Blind" José's wife, made a mistake. She gave him all the medicine at once, and then the laxative. The old man died. Autopsy: poisoned.

There was a little black girl, Isolina, who knew how to read. She was sought after to read the prescriptions. I envied Lina! And I thought, "Ah! I'm gonna learn how to read, too, God willing! If she's black and learned why can't I learn?"

I doubted my potential because the *doutores* from Coimbra said that blacks didn't have the ability. Could that be persecution? What harm had the blacks done to the Portuguese? Why did they hate us, if the blacks were poor and unable to compete with them in anything? That criticism gave the blacks an inferiority complex.

But, there was Mr. Manoel Nogueira who encouraged the blacks. He said, "Mr. Benedito, send your children to school. It's good to know how to read. You should obey Rui Barbosa. He was your friend. Like José do Patrocínio,[5] like Castro Alves.[6] He wrote a book asking clemency for you, who were snatched from your birthplace, which is Africa."

Grandpa would come home from work, eat dinner, and go to hear Mr. Manoel Nogueira read about the things that were happening in the world. Europe was shattered by the war of 1914.

I thought, "If war doesn't benefit men, why do they make war? Can it be that men don't like each other? They mustn't like each other, because they mutually exterminate each other. It is a time when man's mind metamorphoses. He stops being human to become an animal. Could it be that they are unmoved by the blood of their fellow men? And by those who are maimed? And men say that they are the masters of the world. That they are superior. They're always deifying themselves. And men consider themselves civilized. The only man who condemns and disapproves of war is the Pope. And he isn't married. He doesn't have sons who would go fight."

I wanted to ask Mr. Manoel Nogueira who it is who knew everything that was in the newspaper. He had explained that the newspaper was printed in São Paulo. Uncle Cirineu asked him, "Where's São Paulo?"

The black man, Fidêncio, said, "It's another country. You just have to cross the Grande River, you enter Rifama, and then you're in São Paulo."

Mr. Manoel Nogueira scratched his head and said, "Yes . . . Rui was right. It's necessary to educate this people."

---

5. José Carlos do Patrocínio (1854–1905), a journalist and orator. He was an abolitionist and a Republican, he helped runaway slaves and promoted the abolitionist movement in Brazil. In 1892 he was deported to Amazonas because of his liberal ideas.

6. Castro Alves (1847–1871) was a Romantic poet who wrote against slavery and the slave trade. Carolina is probably referring to his famous poems "African Voices" (*"Vozes D'África"*) and "The Slave Ship" (*"Navio Negreiro"*), both of which protest against the horrors of slavery.

What impressed me was the faith that the people put in the man who governed Brazil. It was Doutor Artur Bernardes here, Doutor Artur Bernardes there. They said he had a mixed-up administration, with constitutional guarantees suspended. But, he acted wisely.

Because the powerful people despised him, he dedicated himself to the poor who are much easier to please. The first thing he did was distribute school uniforms, shoes, and books to the poor children. Children who were wearing shoes for the first time smiled, and said, "Artur gave them to me."

And an educational fund was instituted. All of Brazil was moved by this gesture. It was the first time that the people received something from an administration. And how many Our Fathers and Hail Marys the common people prayed so that God would protect the President!

And the ignorant rabble said that President Artur Bernardes had been a student of Saint Vincent de Paul and Saint Anthony of Padua. Mr. Manoel Nogueira laughed, because he was the only one who knew history. And he explained that it wasn't true. Saint Vincent was French, and he was born in 1581 and died in 1660. But the rumor was already spreading by word of mouth. And the President became known as the student of Saint Vincent.

"Oh! So that's why nobody can overthrow him!"

Mr. Manoel Nogueira said, "This people needs intensive study in order to speak knowledgeably and not to speak pretentiously. Whoever speaks knowledgeably is teaching. Our territory is immense, everyone should study in order to protect Brazil and cultivate our lands."

A farmworker made three thousand réis a day. In order to attract men to the countryside, Doutor Artur Bernardes ordered the landowners to pay nine thousand réis a day. Bingo! Who didn't want to be a farmworker? The town was cleaned out.

Men who worked in the city envied the farmworker who received fifty-four thousand réis every Saturday. They had money to spend on their families and their mistresses. And the men were happy because they could have two women.

On Monday, they left the city at dawn, in order to get to the countryside at six in the morning. The men had to get up before the sun appeared in the sky. If they got up later, they were criticized by their friends, "He's soft, he doesn't like to get up early."

Each one got his hoe. They worked, commenting, "I slept with a white woman."

The other one would say, "I slept with a little black girl, and I gave her five thousand réis."

"I gave the white woman ten."

"What's a white woman like?"

"What's a black woman like?"

And each one gave his opinion. "I always said I couldn't die without being with a white woman."

"You see how world is getting better, we black men can sleep with white women now. Equality is coming."

Another one talked about the dance. That he danced with Quirina and squeezed her in his arms, that a fat woman is soft.

A rumor began to spread that a military policeman was making one hundred eighty thousand réis a month. And it wasn't necessary to know how to read. Men began to wonder if they should become military policemen or continue working in the fields.

The military police were fascinating. They could go to the circus and not pay. Sleep with whores and not pay them. Travel by train and not pay, and the government even gave them clothing, room, and board. And some went to be military policemen. They traveled to Uberaba.

The president found out that another revolution was going to break out. When Isidoro started the revolution, the people already adored and venerated president Artur Bernardes. And the people said, "The president didn't go into politics merely to leave his name in history, he'll leave accomplishments."

He promised the people he would create labor laws. They say that he even wrote them. He didn't make them public because of the opposition of the press. They say that the law he formulated is different from the current one. The best salary would be for the farmworker. His objective was to ease crowding in the big cities.

Brazil was famous for being the country of abundance. And Italy bought rice from Brazil and there wasn't enough rice for the people. And the sale of the rice was the Achilles' heel of president Artur Bernardes, because the powerful minority intended to depose him.

But the people were indebted to the president. In every poor home there was a child who adored the president. He was the first philanthropic president of Brazil. He explained that he wouldn't export domestic products any more without consulting the Minister of Agriculture, and apologized to the people.

Rice cost four hundred réis, five hundred réis, or six hundred réis a kilogram. And after that export, it went up to eight hundred réis. And people said: a government that allows the prices of basic necessities to rise isn't a friend of its people. Oh, my God! We were going to starve to death. Nietzsche's prophecies are coming true. In 1870, the German philosopher said, "Ninety years from now, there will be a chaotic transformation in the world. Because business keeps gradually adding a few cents to prices. In 1970, bread will cost one hundred thousand réis a loaf. Pity the man living in 1990."

In Friedrich Nietzsche's time, one hundred thousand réis was the wage of four upper-class men. He was criticized. People said he was crazy. No one believed in this coffee-house philosophy. Nietzsche answered, "Somebody in 1980 will see I was right, and they will applaud me."

The intellectuals of the time said that, from 1970 to 1990, man would be super-man. Love would prevail, there would be no thieves. Men would already be super-civilized. They would be stronger physically and spiritually. There would be no wars, no racial prejudice, and man would not kill his fellow man. Because every person who dies is missed by someone. They wouldn't let prices subjugate them, they would work things out with meetings and not with weapons. They would be very advanced in medicine. Everyone would have a profession. Begging would be nonexistent.

Nobody wanted to read Nietzsche's works, they said he was a moron. The press said that the German writer was imitating Dr. Miguel Nostradamus, the French prophet born in 1503. But Friedrich Nietzsche said, "Somebody from the year 1980 will congratulate me and rehabilitate my memory. I say this with the intention of warning the wretches of that time."

The old people said, "These predictions are going to come true from 1980 to 1990. By then, we'll already be dead. Our commitment is to these poor people. Founding several schools to educate them. And, God willing, they'll have the strength to prepare a Brazil for the Brazilians." Because Rui said that this magnificent Brazil that he envisioned would come about there were no longer illiterate people in our land. That fuel moved motors and knowledge moves man.

In order to calm the people, the president said the cost of living should always be fictional and not reality, and should be within the reach of all.

After the harvest, rice went back to its former price.

At the end of Mr. Artur Bernardes's administration, many children were literate. The poor finished the fourth grade and received a diploma. The rich children went on with their studies. The poor didn't have any chance to go even to high school. How many poor children cried because they wanted to study! And how many rich children cried because they didn't want to study. And they said, "God gives nuts to those who have no teeth."

And those children had no way of learning a trade. If they went to work with Fiúta, they learned cabinet making. Others went to work in the fields. Others went into the Navy. Others went into the Army. To me, the world was like a bottle rack full of bottles where it is difficult to find a place to put more.

Mr. Artur Bernardes was the golden crutch of the lower class. And the people, knowing how to read, were now able to follow the dates on the calendar and know what year it was. The only year the people didn't forget was 1914, because of the war.

After President Artur Bernardes left office, the people would say that his administration was a time of abundance. What I noticed was that, even if salaries were higher, the poor still continued to be poor.

The Italians and the Syrians who had come to Brazil abandoned the crops and went to work in business. The Syrians didn't work in Brazilian agriculture. When the landowners saw their coffee plantations abandoned, they were panic-stricken. There was no one left to work in the fields. They started to beg the blacks to be farmhands.

The blacks went, but the landowners didn't allow them to plant rice around the edges of the coffee plantations. They couldn't plant beans among the coffee, they couldn't raise chickens or pigs; only exclusively care for the coffee. The landowner would give a voucher for one hundred fifty thousand réis to the farmworker, so he could buy food at the local market. The farmworker bought beans, flour, salt, pork, sugar, kerosene, matches, tobacco, soap, and dried meat. He didn't buy rice because there wasn't enough money. What he bought wouldn't last eight days. And if he asked for another voucher, he had to hear this, "You guys work very little and eat a lot."

At the end of the year, the landowner would settle accounts with the black man, and the black man owed him five hundred thousand réis . . .

Only the Italians were allowed to plant among the coffee, and they sold their surplus produce. And the landowner paid them to take care of the coffee crop.

The black man lost interest in the life of a farmworker, and fled the farms, taking with him only a bundle of clothes. His belongings stayed on the farm. He returned to the city. He would get some kind of job and live in the Italians' basement, or in a shack.

I heard only rumors that the Portuguese had fought desperately to be the masters of these lands. But I didn't see any Portuguese in the fields. They only valued Brazil while the Africans were working for free to make them rich. When they had to pay for the services the blacks performed, they lost interest in Brazil. They didn't go to work in the fields. And they cursed blacks, "Lazy niggers, if there were still slavery with laborers to work for free, Brazil would still be a Portuguese colony."

But, José Bonifácio,[7] José do Patrocínio, Castro Alves, Luiz Gama,[8] the Baron of Rio Branco[9] didn't accept slavery.

In 1922, Brazil had already been discovered for 422 years. And people said, "Backward country!"

It wasn't the country, it was its inhabitants who had no chance to educate themselves.

I asked my mother, "Why is the world so confusing?"

She answered me, "The world is a house that belongs to several owners, if one sweeps it, another one comes to get it dirty."

But it's just like that. A man only values his fellow man after he dies. If men govern the world, it's never a good place for people to live in, why not let women govern? Women wouldn't make war, because they are men's mothers. But men are men's fathers, they make war and kill each other.

My mother said that she wouldn't let me go hear Mr. Manoel Nogueira read any more, that I was going crazy. She suggested I go play with my dolls. It didn't appeal to me. I wasn't interested. I

---

7. José Bonifácio de Andrada e Silva (1763–1838) was one of the main advocates of Brazilian independence in 1822.

8. Luís Gonzaga de Pinto Gama (1830–1882) was a former slave who became a lawyer and specialized in defending slaves in court.

9. José Maria da Silva Paranhos Júnior, the Baron of Rio Branco (1845–1912), was a diplomat who negotiated border disputes with Bolivia and Peru, and set modern foreign policy goals for Brazil. Moreover, he developed a modernization and industrialization plan for the nation.

couldn't live peacefully in this world that's like a messy house. Oh! If only it were possible for me to fight to straighten it up!

I saw people die and thought, "What is the use of man being born if, when he finally learns to live in the world, he's old and dies?"

I observed men's actions. The blacks drank a lot of *pinga*. When a child was born, they drank because they were happy. But that child who was born would live just like them when he grew up. When they were sad, they drank *pinga*. But the result of drinking *pinga* was getting drunk, fighting, killing each other, then being arrested and beaten up by the military policemen. And I thought, "I will never drink *pinga*. And I will always keep all the promises I make to myself."

I observed the consequences of everything we do. When the blacks drank, I thought, "Why do only blacks drink?" But the whites drank at home. If a white man staggered through the streets, they would say he was indisposed, he wasn't feeling well. If a white man drank in the bars, he was reprimanded, "Are you imitating the blacks? Did you get a black man to be your teacher? The only thing a black man can teach us is how to drink *pinga*. When it comes to *pinga,* they are the experts."

When there was a fight, it was the black man who was arrested. And many times, the black guy was only watching. The military police couldn't arrest the whites, so they arrested the blacks. Having white skin was a protection, a safe-passage.

And Mr. Manoel Nogueira said, "What injustice! But I don't have the nerve to interfere. I am a half-breed in the human race. My father is white. My mother is black. I need to defend my mother's brothers. They have the right to live and be happy, these hostilities because of color are a sign of mediocrity. It's the primitivism of the powerful."

He said that, for Rui, when the blacks learned how to read, they would know how to defend themselves. They won't humbly accept the yoke. Even a dog can defend itself. It knows how to snarl to demand respect. They are not going to accept impositions. Rui said that in Brazil there will yet be black *doutores,* physicians, lawyers, engineers, and even teachers. Brazil won't always be like this. The men of the future will be more cultured. These rotten despots will die. Blacks should study and not be resentful. The legacy of hate shouldn't be passed down from father to son. "I won't live to see these things Rui prophesied. But you, when you're hired as servants, shouldn't steal from your bosses. The servant will associate with the boss's relatives.

He has to obey and respect him. Sometimes a man struggles to find a job. When he gets one, he gets lazy. Blacks shouldn't kill whites. Whites shouldn't kill blacks. Blacks and whites have to dance a quadrille. Stand *vis-à-vis*[10] all over Brazil."

I was already sick of hearing "black and white." I thought men should talk less and work more. They should imitate the Japanese who came from Japan. They talk very little and work a lot.

---

10. Carolina herself uses the French expression *vis-à-vis,* literally "face to face."

6

The Blacks

"If only I could buy this! If only I could buy that!"

I would wear one of my mother's dresses, tie a rope around my waist, and jump over the neighbor's wall, climb the trees, pick fruit, put it in the bodice of the dress, then, I would come down and go enjoy it.

But I didn't have inner peace. My conscience warned me that I had done a shameful thing. I didn't have the nerve to steal. I must and will fight to get everything honestly. I had the feeling that somebody was whispering in my ears, "be honest, be honest, be honest," as if it were the tick-tock of a clock. It seemed that I had a mentor guiding me. When I was given a piece of fruit, or I bought one, I didn't get frightened, everyone has common sense. If a man steals, it's because he's rotten.

After a few days, I decided to go into my neighbor's garden. When I went to pick a mango, a snake was just putting his mouth on it. I was startled, lost my balance, and fainted. I went tumbling down from top to bottom, hitting against the branches, and fell to the ground, almost unconscious. I forgot I was stealing mangos. I started to wail, the dogs, hearing me wail, barked, and the chickens cackled. Dona Faustina came to see what was going on. She found me with my bodice stuffed with mangos. She gave me a look that terrified me. I realized that she was stingy.

She scolded me! "So, it's you who's stealing my fruit. Lazy little nigger. Niggers are worthless."

I answered, "Whites are thieves, too, because they stole the blacks from Africa."

She looked at me with disgust. "As if I would go to Africa to bring you . . . I don't like monkeys."

I thought Africa was the mother of the blacks. Poor Africa who, when she arrived home, didn't find her children. She must have cried a lot.

I was lying on the ground and saying, "Watch out for the snake! Watch out for the snake!" I fainted.

They went to tell my mother I was stealing Dona Faustina's mangos. My mother got a whip and gave me two lashes. I woke up and went running off, as if my legs were motorized.

My mother was furious because I had put on her new dress. It was a cotton print dress. What torment when I walked down the streets and the children shouted, "Mango thief! Mango thief."

But those were incidents that passed. And children soon forget what they see and the days went by.

I noticed that whites were more calm because they already had their livelihood. And for the blacks, because they didn't have any education, life was more difficult. When they found work, it was exhausting. My seventy-three-year-old grandfather picked up boulders for the stonecutters to make into the foundations of houses. Blacks, when they received their pittance, didn't know how to spend it on useful things. They spent it buying *pinga.* Blacks were terrified of the police, who harassed them. Those scenes reminded me of cats running away from dogs.

The whites, who were Brazil's masters, didn't defend the blacks. They only smiled, finding it funny to see the blacks running from one place to another. Looking for cover, in order not to be hit by a bullet.

My great-grandmother Maria Abadia used to say, "The whites today treat blacks better. Now, they shoot to scare them, they used to shoot to kill them."

And the blacks smiled saying, "Benedito ran like a rabbit when he saw the police."

When the blacks said, "Now we are free," I thought, "But what kind of freedom is this, if they have to run from the authorities as if they were guilty of a crime? So, the world used to be worse for blacks?

Then, the world is black for the blacks and white for the whites!''
I noticed that they didn't mess much with the black women. They
didn't make them run. But, they said dirty words to them and showed
their penis, and I went to tell my mother, ''You know, Mama, I saw a
man showing his 'candle' to Vitalina, and he said some things that I
didn't understand. Vitalina's daughter cried and said she's gonna tell
her boyfriend.''

When it didn't rain, the women got together and went on pilgrim-
ages, to pray at the feet of the crosses, and wash the crosses, and ask
God to send rain, they lit candles.[1] My grandfather prayed the rosary.
Whoever knew how to pray was treated with special deference. He
received invitations to go pray in distant places. After the rosary, we
drank pineapple liqueur, and there were various refreshments. Corn
pone, manioc flour cookies. I was proud of being the granddaughter of
a man who knew how to pray the rosary, convinced that we were
important. I preferred rice pudding prepared with pure milk.

My grandfather's eight children didn't know how to read. They
worked as unskilled laborers. My grandfather was disappointed because his children hadn't learned to read, and said, ''It wasn't my fault.
It's that at the time his children should have studied, schools for blacks
weren't open. When you go to school, study hard and strive to learn.''
And we, the grandchildren, received Grandpa's words as if they were a
kiss and a caress.

My grandfather was a shadow who had left the slave quarters
broken and disillusioned, recognizing that he had worked to make his
Portuguese master rich. Because those who were born here in Brazil
were disgusted to live by exploiting the blacks.

Grandpa said that the Brazilians were good men, pure of mind,
like the clouds in the sky. ''God help the men of Brazil,'' and he
cried, saying, ''The man who is born a slave is born crying, lives
crying, and dies crying. When they kicked us off the plantations, we
didn't have a decent roof over our heads, if we settled in some
corner, that place already belonged to someone, the caretakers drove
us away. When someone assisted us, we knew at once that that was
a Brazilian soul. And we had faith: the men who fought to emanci-
pate us will make a place for us, what we have going for us is that

---

1. According to Câmara Cascudo, it is traditional to wash the crosses in order
to ask for rain during long droughts.

we all die someday, and, on the other side, there are no color distinctions, there, the good works we do here will prevail.''

In the month of August, when the nights were hotter, we gathered around Grandpa to hear him tell about the horrors of slavery. He talked about Palmares, the famous *quilombo*,[2] where the blacks sought refuge. The leader was a courageous black man named Zumbi.[3] He intended to liberate the blacks. There was a decree: whoever killed Zumbi would earn two hundred thousand réis and the title of ''baron.'' But, where did you ever see a hired killer get a title of nobility! A nobleman, to be worth anything, must have education and lineage.

But, with so much fuss around blacks, blacks were becoming important, blacks and gold were things of great value. And with the debates, emancipation or no emancipation, the Portuguese were becoming more friendly to the blacks. But they didn't manage to regain their trust, and they were already weakening. If they were hard on the blacks, they were criticized, losing their authority.

The abolitionists incited the blacks not to obey the masters. Even if they wanted to start an uprising, they would be alone, they couldn't count on the cooperation of their slaves. They started to give presents to the slaves. They would pierce the little black girls' ears, they would offer them gold earrings with the intent of regaining their trust. But, there had already been almost four hundred years of suffering.[4]

There were blacks who died at twenty-five: of sadness, because they were sick of being sold. Today they were here, tomorrow there, as if they were leaves scattered by the wind. They envied the trees that were born, grew, and died in the same place. Blacks aren't immigrants, they are settlers. They don't dream of other shores. Sometimes, a man was sold and separated from his wife. The masters had

---

2. *Quilombos* were small communities formed by runaway slaves. The largest and most famous one was Palmares, located in the interior of the state of Alagoas. Palmares reached a population of 200,000 inhabitants in the seventeenth century before being destroyed by Portuguese military expeditions at the end of that century.

3. Zumbi was the most famous leader of Palmares and was killed in 1695.

4. This passage is ambiguous in the Portuguese. In places, the pronouns Carolina uses make it unclear to whom she is referring. This ambiguity has been preserved in the translation.

spread the word that they were damned by the prophet Ham.[5] That they were to have black skin, and be slaves of the whites. Slavery was like a scar on the black man's soul.

When a black man said, "I'm free!" nobody believed him, and they made fun of him. "A snake was going to bite my master, I saw it and killed it and my master said that I had saved his life and freed me. Now I'm the apple of my master's eye. I have lunch at the same table at the master's side, and I don't sleep in the slave quarters."

After emancipation, the Portuguese were terrified of the blacks. It was the other side of the coin for those who had been lions and were forced to become lambs. Thousands of people left the country and Brazil was adrift. "Since you are free, get off my land! Let's see if you manage to fill your bellies with freedom. Just imagine, having to give money to niggers! It's a sin!"

The people were angry because their dream was to learn to read, in order to read Castro Alves's book. The blacks silently adored Tiradentes.[6] If a black man mentioned Tiradentes's name, he was beaten, and sent to the whipping post as an example. To the Portuguese, Tiradentes was the devil's secretary. To the blacks, he was God's minister.

Grandpa looked at us with tenderness, "God protected them, helping them not to be born during the time of slavery." The freed blacks couldn't stay in the same place. They had to leave their cities. Some went to the state of Rio, others to the state of Minas, of Goiás, in order to be free of the curses of the former masters, and they repeated Castro Alves's words, "A black man is free when he dies."

I was five years old, I thought those antagonistic scenes were strange, my embryonic mind didn't help me to understand those conflicts. If a black man walked by with his head hanging down, the white man cursed! "Lazy nigger! I don't like this race! I used to have this race working for me."

And I thought, "My God! Who was it who started this question, was it the blacks or was it the whites? Who went looking for the

---

5. See Gen. 9: 18-26 and Gen. 10 for the story of Noah's son, Ham. The story of Ham's sin has been used to justify the enslaving of dark-skinned peoples.

6. Tiradentes, literally "toothpuller," was the nickname of Joaquim José da Silva Xavier (1756-1792), one of the leaders of the Inconfidência Mineira, a failed rebellion against Portuguese rule that took place in 1788-1789. The Inconfidência Mineira was one of the first efforts toward Brazil's independence from Portugal.

blacks? If it was the whites who went looking for the blacks, they have no right to complain. The blacks didn't invade their lands, they were the ones who invaded the blacks' lands.'' There was nobody to explain it to me. My mother was already fed up with my questions.

But the world is so big! There is so much space, everybody can live well here! Why these fights? My grandfather said, ''Those who fight are animals, that don't know how to think.''

So, man is an animal because he fights more than the animals. Oh, my God! If the world is like that, it isn't worth it to be born! If civility doesn't prevail among men, they will never be happy. There is more hatred in the world than friendship.

I already knew that the persecuted races in the world were: the Blacks, because of their color; the Gypsies, for being nomads, swindling thieves, and having no homeland; and the Semites, because they had fought with Christ. But if Christ, who was offended and martyred, forgave them, then why is it that men hold a grudge? If only men, after Christ's death, had stopped killing, understanding the uselessness of man killing his fellow man! But, man continued in his perversion. He doesn't respect the Ten Commandments governing free will. When one man kills another, he becomes boastful, arrogant.

My Aunt Claudimira worked for Syrians who had come to Brazil as immigrants. And here they even had servants. She made thirty thousand réis a month, for washing clothes, ironing them, taking care of the children, the house, and the kitchen.

I thought, ''Why could it be that they leave their homeland and come to Brazil?'' And they say that our country is a little piece of heaven. There was no reason to hate them, because they liked the country, and didn't bother anyone. I thought, ''Can it be that Brazil will always be good like they say? Why is it that foreigners arrive here poor and get rich? And we, the natives are born here, here we live and die poor?''

I heard it said that the foreigners who have been in Brazil longer helped the poor countrymen. That the rich Brazilians don't help the poor Brazilian, they don't trust him. The foreigners didn't come poor. They weren't illiterate and they dominated trade. And the illiterate Brazilian didn't have any means of progressing.

My aunt brought *kibbe*[7] for us to eat, and she said that the Syrians

---

7. Middle Eastern meat patties.

ground the meat in a mortar. And we laughed. Brazilians weren't familiar with lentils, and they said they were Turkish beans.

If someone asked, "Are you Turkish?"

"No, I Syrian! Turks are worthless!"

I thought, "What kind of a world is this? A world that it's necessary to have lots of patience to live in."

The Japanese said, "The Chinese are no good."

The Chinese said, "The Japanese no good."

The whites said, "Yellow people are worthless."

The whites said, "Blacks are worthless."

The blacks said, "Yellow people are worthless, and whites are worthless, too."

White people created high society and blacks don't get into it. Only the earth has no pride. In this world, humanity is born and dies. When a man is alive, he lives off the grains that come from the earth. And when he dies, he goes to the earth's bosom. She doesn't speak, but she is wise. She is God's best work.

I liked fruit, but it was hard to get money to buy it. I was already realizing that the poor lived with more dreams.

One day, I heard my mother telling that my Uncle Joaquim was drinking water from a public tap—the fountain—when Juca Barão's son came up and said to him, "Get out of here, dirty nigger! I should drink first because I'm white," and he pushed my uncle, who got upset and pulled out a little knife that he made from a barrel hoop, and struck a blow on the nape of Juca Barão's son's neck, and he fell lifeless to the ground.

My uncle wasn't arrested because he was a minor.

The judge was Doutor Brand. The whites got together and went to curse Grandpa, "Now that blacks are free, they're going to kill the whites and they are protected by the law."

These incidents were an excuse for the Portuguese to claim, "These savage acts are the consequence of freedom. And you are going to see worse things, since Rui even said that, if a black man studies, he will be able to be governor, president, a representative, senator, and even a diplomat."

The blacks who heard didn't answer because the Portuguese were rich. They were free, but poor. In confrontations between blacks and whites, no one tries to figure out who is right. And the black man always ends up being the scape-goat.

7

My Family

My grandfather was the father of eight children. Four men and four women.

The men were: José Benedito, Antônio, Joaquim, João Benedito.

João had meningitis as a child, he was left with an atrophied brain. Joaquim was the family's champion, we called him Tróhem.

The women: Maria Carolina, Maria Verônica, Ana, and Claudimira.

Aunt Ana, "Donda" was her nickname, married a mulatto, Cândido Nunes. She left a son, Adão Nunes.

Aunt Ana died of *barriga d'água.*[1] It was Dr. Vicente Cândido dos Santos who discovered the illness. And he operated on her. When the water poured into the basin, I stood staring at that green water without understanding the weaknesses of the human body. And Dr. Vicente became famous.

My aunt was unhappy in her marriage. That's what I heard said, that her husband was no friend of work. When someone advised him to get a job, he scratched his head as if in that gesture he were looking for a solution to his problems. What he really liked to do was sit and talk.

---

1. Abdominal edema, an abnormal accumulation of fluid in the abdominal cavity, causing a swelling of the area. This is a common illness among Brazil's poor because it is caused by parasites.

He told marvelous stories. If he knew how to read, he could be a great writer. He wasn't pornographic.

My Aunt Claudimira was beautiful when she was young. Wherever she went she heard this: "What beauty! What a beautiful woman." She became vain. She had several suitors. But none was good enough. She found defects in all of them. And time was going by.

My naïve aunt thought that youth and beauty are a long-lasting pair. A woman should marry when she is young. She was getting older, and she had settled in at the age of eighteen. Thus began my aunt's calvary, she didn't want to die without knowing a man's caresses.

When the women got together to talk about the pleasures that men give to a woman, she always listened. Regretting her foolishness. She, who had the opportunity to get married, to have a home, and she didn't get married. And her aging presence no longer excited men. Children whom she had seen born and grow up, passed the age of eighteen, and my aunt remained restricted to eighteen. As if it were an irremovable mountain.

I looked at my Uncle Joaquim's face. A face sad as a moonless night. He didn't smile, I never saw his teeth. He was illiterate. If he knew how to read, he could show us his intellectual qualities.

Now my Uncle Antônio was a happier guy. I remember that he went to have his picture taken by the photographer João Bianchi. The portrait came out dark. You could only make out his white suit coat. My uncle cursed, "I'm not as black as that. Everything that you all do for blacks is careless. But if the white man pays, the black man also pays. And I'm not going to pay."

An argument began, "Pay!" "Not pay!" João Bianchi said, "Dio mio. If you black, it not possible that portrait be white."

My uncle paid, cursing.

The woman who lived with my grandfather was Siá Maruca. A calm black woman. They were an elegant couple. When they spoke, if Grandpa reproached her, she cried and bowed her head and apologized. When Grandpa wasn't around I said, "Siá Maruca, why is it that you don't react when Grandpa criticizes you?"

"No, my dear! The woman should obey the man."

I became furious. And I cried because I wanted to become a man so that women would obey me.

We called my Uncle Manoel "Bass Manoel" because of his baritone voice. His children, known as "the Basses" were eight, four men and four women.

Rosa went crazy when she was seduced by a man who refused to marry her. My Uncle Manoel had an *azagaia*.[2] A weapon in the shape of a leaf. It was a gift from his grandfather, who got it in the war with Paraguay. It cuts on both sides.

Aunt Jerônima, my mother's aunt, was so poor that it was pitiful, she had only one pan. She got up at three in the morning and put the beans on. While the beans cooked, she seasoned them, and poured them out into a wooden bowl. She made the rice and poured it out into another wooden bowl, finally, she made the vegetables and ate from the little wooden bowls. The spoons she ate with were also wooden.

My aunt prayed, asking God to help her preserve that pan. And if that pan broke, what would become of them? What pity I felt for Aunt Jerônima! If I could only give her some pans, but I was also poor. She didn't have anything to wear. The beds were made of poles buried in the ground. The mattress was made of an old cotton sack, and the blankets, too. It seemed like a recreation of the manger of Bethlehem.

My Aunt Ana Marcelina, my maternal grandmother's sister, was a light mulatta. The classic mulatta. She didn't like blacks. She paid more attention to whites. When she looked at blacks, it was with semi-closed eyes and she turned her gaze aside. Although Aunt Ana didn't like blacks, she had a black son, Mindu. Mindu's real name was Octaviano. What a handsome black man! He was a cabinet maker.

I have very little to say about this aunt because she was a mulatta. And there was, like a wall between the families, racial prejudice. My aunt wore fine clothes just like those of the whites. She strove to live just like the rich. She lived in a comfortable house. On all the doors and windows, there were curtains. There were carpets. The beds were curtained. They ate at the table.

Her daughters liked to dance. They didn't go to the whites' dances because they weren't invited. They didn't want to go to the blacks' dances. When we, the black nieces and nephews, went to visit her, we weren't allowed to enter. Blacks don't enter the houses of mulattos.

My mother was born in the country. On the banks of the Velhas River. When she grew up, they went to live in the city. My mother

---

2. A small spear-like weapon.

married Mr. Osório Pereira. My mother and her husband were separated. She complained, "Osorio married me to get out of his guardianship." His guardian was Mr. Miguel Alvim. One of the rich families, one of those who raised foundlings to take care of the pigs, chickens, sweep the house, pick up, cook, and go shopping. Owning slaves was prohibited, so they got little black children to raise them. An unfortunate who was going to grow up with no education.

When Mr. Osório Pereira married my mother, his guardian gave him only five hundred thousand réis. He didn't give him a piece of land so he could build his little house. He gave him a pair of used pants. And some pairs of shoes so big that my mother's husband would have to cut the shoes in half or else double his feet. The pants were huge because Mr. Alvim was obese.

My mother told me that Mr. Osório looked like an earthworm in the pants. She complained that her marriage wasn't based on love. It was business. He wanted to be free of his guardianship, he was fed up with that confined life he lived.

Mr. Osório Pereira kept spending the money, thinking that those five hundred thousand réis were inexhaustible. It was the first time that he had money to spend, he could have bought a house. When the money ran out, he became furious. He hadn't bought anything to eat, and he didn't know what he had spent the money on. He had to look for work. He regretted having gotten married. In Mr. Miguel Alvim's house he had food and a room in which to sleep.

One day, as they had nothing to eat, he said, "Maria, give me a bag because I'm going to buy a beef rib so you can make some soup." My mother lit the fire and put on water to boil. She was happy when she spied her husband, "Thank God, I'm going to have a husband who will help me to bear the weight of my life." Her husband arrived and spilled out the contents of the bag. They were coconuts, and he said to her, "The butcher refused to sell me the bones on credit, and he even called me Osório Cricket. I don't know what he meant by that. Let's eat coconuts until I get a job."

My mother went to complain to Grandpa, and he lent her two thousand réis, "Where did you ever hear of supporting a home with coconuts." They began losing interest in each other.

My mother was semi-free. If a woman worked to help her husband, people said, "Good Lord. Where did you ever see a married woman working! She should only work in her home." Despite the gossip, my mother went to work. With a lot of freedom, my mother danced and spent the nights with her friends, and she became intoxicated with the affection of her *bangulê*[3] friends.

It was at one of these questionable dances that she met my father. They say that he was a very handsome black man. He played the guitar and composed improvised verses. He was known as the Bohemian poet. At the dances, he only danced with my mother. She had only one son with her husband, Jerônimo Pereira. The last name Pereira, my mother's husband's, must have been inherited from some Portuguese because my mother's husband was mulatto. When my mother got pregnant, there arose a lot of gossip, which was so common in the towns in the countryside.

The tongues of country people in small towns are sharp, they are bigger than the sea and faster than thoughts. Destructive tongues that have pulled down many ideals, tongues that sometimes hit the mark, and sometimes miss.

They said that the child who was going to be born was the daughter of the Bohemian poet. When I was born, the rumors were confirmed, and the evil tongues felt they were almost prophetic. My resemblance to the poet served as a pretext for my mother's husband to abandon her.

He was the irresponsible kind of man who doesn't support his home, and demands fidelity. He wasn't old enough to be the head of a family. What he wanted was to get married to get his freedom. He wasn't fair to my mother, caring for her, watching out for her happiness. He said, "I married a black woman only to get out of my guardianship."

And he went to live with a white woman. An old lady of fifty-two, she could be his grandmother. But she was white. And he said that a white woman was ageless, "She's always young."

My mother was left with two children to support. My mother told me that she drank numerous cures in order to abort me, and she didn't manage to. Finally, she gave up and decided to raise me. I wasn't sad or mad, perhaps it would be better not to exist. Because I was already

---

3. According to John T. Schneider's *Dictionary of African Borrowings in Brazilian Portuguese* (Hamburg: Buske, 1991), *bangulê* is an African dance accompanied by the *cuica* (a hand-held percussion instrument), hand clapping, stomping, and obscene songs.

understanding that the world isn't a bed of roses. There is always something to enslave you.

When she went to work, she left me in the care of Siá Maruca. They say that I cried day and night. And my endless crying irritated Siá Maruca and the neighbors who said, "Doesn't she get tired of crying? Does she think she's pleasing us? She's relentless."[4] And Siá Maruca was mad because I stopped her from taking care of her work, which was washing clothes at three hundred réis a dozen. Oh! That daily crying. I was making her crazy. She was very timid and good, and didn't have the nerve to complain to my mother in order not to displease Grandpa, who said, "It is a man's responsibility to accept his grandchildren, legitimate or illegitimate, and tolerate his children's faults."

One day, she gave me *pinga* to drink. I fell asleep and didn't cry. Siá Maruca smiled saying, "I found the cure for you. You want *pinga*, little scoundrel!" When my mother arrived home from work, not hearing my crying, she went to investigate. I was unconscious. My mother grabbed me and took me to the Spiritualist doctor Mr. Eurípedes Barsanulfo. He looked and me, smiled, and told her, "She's drunk, they gave her alcohol so she would drink and fall asleep." My mother complained that I cried day and night. He said that my skull didn't have enough space to hold my brains, that they were squeezed, and I got a headache. He explained to her that, until I was twenty-one, I would live as if I were dreaming, that my life would be confused. She's going to love everything that's beautiful! Your daughter is a poet; poor Sacramento, from your breast comes a poet. And he smiled. He gave me some medicine to make me throw up the alcohol, and said with an energetic voice, "You . . . you're never to drink. Alcohol is a very poor support. Because I'm always going to help you."

I remember when I got the mumps. The boil burst. My mother squeezed it to get out the pus. I cried. We were at a wake. I was sitting on my mother's lap, so happy with that show of affection.

It was a couple who had died from not being able to love each other

---

4. The Portuguese expression Carolina uses here, *fôlego de gato,* literally means "cat's breath." It describes someone who has a lot of physical endurance, who can keep up strenuous physical activity for a long time. This follows from what Câmara Cascudo says about the cat in Brazilian popular tradition: it has the reputation for being agile and quick, and having multiple lives.

freely due to a family restriction. The woman who died was the daughter of Aunt Ana, the mulatta who didn't like blacks. She was my mother's cousin. No one in the family would notice the indifference with which Aunt Ana treated us. But I noticed it. I hated those little intrigues people made up, mental pigmies, and I thought, "Why could it be that mulattos and whites reject blacks?" From the whites it's even acceptable! But the mulatto? He's in the middle. He's the son of a black and the son of a white. The races that unite to produce the mulatto. The mulatto can't attack the white man. Because the white man is white. So, he turns against the black man. But the white man doesn't accept the mulatto as white. There was even a bill saying that, if the mulatto had straight hair, he was considered white, if his hair were kinky, then the mulatto was considered black.

The comments at the wake were insulting to Aunt Ana, who prevented her daughter from marrying a black man. Saying that she wanted her daughter to marry a white man to purify the race. It's that she didn't know that black is a pure race in its origin. And white, too.

Mariinha married a white man, João Miguel, the only thing that this man offered his wife was a life full of suffering. He was an alcoholic. And his wife didn't drink. Their home was the model of misery. It was a black man who supported it. It was horrible to see Mariinha's husband ask the black man for money to drink *pinga* and say, "I hate you, and I hate my wife too, because she loves you." What ignorance of my aunt to accept that worthless man, a guy who was unacceptable even in the most sordid circles, just because of the color of his skin!

When the black man met with Mariinha, he would cry, telling her, "If you were only mine! My life would be happier." Mariinha cried, saying, "João Miguel makes me sick. How horrible the presence of a man is when we don't love him. I shouldn't have been born. Because I wasn't born free, I was born the slave to my mother's vanity." That white daughter was Aunt Ana's pride and joy. She was the favorite.

I thought, "The black shouldn't produce the mulatto because he turns against him. He who gets stabbed is the one who can judge pain. And it's the black man who is able to reveal the vanity and arrogance of the mulattos. The blacks don't persecute the mulatto because he's a mulatto, nor the white man because he's white. Therefore, the black man is the superior one."

Mariinha was always saying, "I'm going to die!" She was the

mother of two sons, Adálio and Olímpio. They were Aunt Ana's first grandchildren. Her white-skinned grandchildren.

The black man said, "Don't say you're going to die, because the day you die, I will also die. I wouldn't be able to stand to live in this world without you. I hope that your suffering serves as a lesson to your mother, who thinks that white-skinned people are almost God! You're not the only one who is dying—I am, too."

When the black man found out that Mariinha had died, he ran out saying, "No! It can't be! She's not going to leave me alone in this world that was bitter for us. But heaven is going to be sweet for us. They are fooling me! This is a trick! If she died, I'm going to sleep in the cemetery, next to her grave."

It was the month of November. It was raining. He ran in the mud that spattered on his clothes. When he saw the body of the woman that he loved so deeply extended inert, he knelt down and cried, "I loved you, with all respect. With all tenderness, dear Maria." He sat down in a chair and cried.

The white husband was in Nicolau's tavern drinking *pinga*.

The people who were present at the wake prayed, and spoke of the wretched life that the deceased had led, commenting that God had done a good thing in taking her away.

Aunt Ana was sad. She had lost her charmed daughter, and she was ashamed of the consequences of her pride. I was already getting used to death because the mortality in the state of Minas Gerais is astonishing.

I thought that it was a disease that was called love. So, this disease kills . . . Could this disease be contagious? When I heard someone talking about love, I said, "Go to the doctor because this disease kills."

"Oh! Idiotic little nigger girl! Nasty little nigger girl." When someone was going to curse me, it was "Little nigger girl! Little nigger girl!"

What chaos when the black man fell down dead. What running about! They went to get the doctor to examine the corpse. The people said, "Wow, he was true to his word, he promised her that, if she died, he would die too, and he really died."

My aunt stopped being a racist for a little while. But when her son João wanted to marry Siá Maruca's daughter, she didn't consent. And Mariinha's death gave the people something to talk about for several months. Finally, Aunt Ana began resigning herself, and didn't interfere any more in her daughters' love-affairs.

Poor Mariinha, she had the misfortune of having white skin that was the cause of her death. She didn't despise blacks. If my aunt were intelligent, she would understand that people's value isn't in their color, it's in their actions. Mariinha used to say, "I wish I had black skin and kinky hair. How beautiful a black face is, with its shining teeth."

It was the most agitated night I ever saw. I heard a woman ask my mother, "What does the little girl have?"

"She has the mumps."

"How old is she?"

"She's four years old."

I thought of asking what "four years old" was. But my mother had said that children can't ask questions at wakes. How horrible it is to be a child. You don't have permission to do this or that. What a world this is, we have to accept restrictions; this being so, man isn't free.

But the grown-ups talked, fought, drank, and even stole. I mean that adults should also have been, and should be, reprimanded, the acts of adults have tragic consequences, as if they had neither faith in God nor a conscience. It was as if they had been born and grown up naked. They never clothed their feelings in goodness. They loved the man Jesus Christ, but they didn't obey his teachings.

Oh! If I could only not grow up! There were times when I was against grown-ups. But there were times when I adored them. When they gave me sweets, meat with bread, milk, cheese, and two thousand réis coins. How I liked those coins. What pretty little money!

As far as men were concerned, I liked the priests because they didn't speak of war. They were pleasant when they spoke with the children who went to catechism class. They said that we should pray to God to help us. The priests were Father Pedro and Father Julião. It was so nice to stay in the church.

When a black man saw a military policeman, he went into the church and knelt at the foot of the altar. He stayed there a few minutes, praying. In the church he was protected. The military policeman wouldn't reprimand, wouldn't interrogate him.

If the men got together, it was to speak of Aunt Ana. They eulogized the deceased daughter, "Let's get together and have a mass said for her."

My mother said that we should respect the dead, that they went to heaven, that it is God who takes us, and they never again return to earth. I lifted my eyes up to the sky to see if I saw the residence of the dead, "Can it be that the dead fight, can the dance hall in heaven be big, or is it canopied? Do the women from up there in heaven sleep with the men? Do the police from heaven beat the blacks? Do the mulattos in heaven not like the blacks?"

And my mother blew up, "Shut up, bitch! Do you want to make me crazy! I don't know anything about heaven, I was never there. Only after I die will I go to heaven. But it must be terrible to die!"

My Aunt Claudimira used to say, "If I were you, I would commit this little black girl to an insane asylum."

"She's my daughter! A woman's mission is to be patient with her children, whether he be a Cain or an Abel."

I thought, "Who could Cain have been? What could he have done? And Abel?"

Siá Maruca gave me a vermifuge. All of the children had to take it. I was horrified when I saw the quantity of worms I expelled, "People have these vermin in their stomachs?"

"They do."

"What do they eat?"

"The food that you eat." And Siá Maruca left to be free of my interrogation.

People cursed Aunt Ana. But she didn't know it. My mother used to tell that she left the wake at ten o'clock because I had the mumps. After she lay down, she heard Mariinha's voice calling, "Cota! Cota, Cota." At midnight, the voice disappeared.

Every week someone would die.

It was rare for a rich person to die because as soon as they got sick, they went for the doctor. By the time a poor person got together the money to go to the doctor, it was already too late.

The doctor who took care of the sick was Dr. Cunha, Dona Leozínia's husband, the most beautiful woman in Sacramento. I didn't want my mother to die because the children who were left without mothers went to live with other families and they lost their freedom.

How the blacks loved the illusion of freedom! They had no support, but they were happy.

Thank God Mama isn't going to die because I don't want to go live with anyone because I would have to work, get beaten, and I wouldn't be able to play. I found out that the children who didn't have mothers were orphans. And I was afraid of the word orphan.

Every Saturday there was a wedding in the city. What rushing around. The women made sweets, cookies, killed chickens, ducks, and turkeys. They borrowed plates, forks, knives, cups, and chairs from the neighbors. They baked cookies in the shape of letters with the names of the bride and groom.

When Jerônima, Siá Dona's daughter, married Jovino, I went to see the wedding. Jerônima was blond, with blue eyes and light hair. Jovino was a mulatto. I looked at Jovino's face. The face of a serious man who would know how to respect that commitment. The marriage took place at home. Because the bride was white and she was ashamed to go through the streets to the notary public's office to marry a mulatto. These rumors circulated, but didn't reach Jovino's ears. The bride was beautiful! And her mother satisfied, saying, "I am already old and thank God I have married my daughter! If I die, she'll look after Claudimira." Who was her younger sister.

The bride's step-father was happy. Even I was happy.

The notary was Mr. José Neto, who said, "You're lucky! You married a beautiful white girl."

After the wedding, the young people went on a trip. They went to the country. And we kept dancing.

I thought, "Why is it that parties always end with dances, dancing isn't necessary." I didn't like to dance. But I learned because I thought it was required. I thought we were required to learn everything that rules the world. But drinking *pinga,* this I didn't want to learn. Stealing, I already knew, was prohibited. Whoever killed a thief didn't go to jail. But many injustices occurred. Sometimes one man killed another and said that the victim was a thief to get out of going to jail.

Time went by. Four years later Jerônima ran away with a white man. Because she was disgusted to have a black mother-in-law. She didn't have any children. She didn't want to, Jovino was left alone.

He had cows, pigs, fields of rice, and many sacks of processed rice and unhulled rice. Several kinds of beans. And eight fat pigs and a harnessed horse so that Jerônima could ride.

Some time later I saw Jovino walking through the streets of Sacramento, and more than one time I looked at that serious face of a good man. It wasn't possible for him to see his dream come true—he wanted children. God was the judge of that union.

My cousins invited me to play. I didn't like to because my hair didn't grow and they said, "Bald head! Bald head, man's head! You're not going to get married ... because men don't marry women who don't have hair."

I used to ask my mother to braid my hair. What pain!

One day, my mother showed me an iron comb saying that the masters made the slaves comb their hair with that kind of comb. Because black hair is coarse. What a horrible comb. It pulled out all the hair.

I saw several blacks who had been rewarded with the Emancipation Law[5] and with freedom. They put up little shacks along the sides of the roads because the sides of public roads belonged to the government and no one said anything. They told of the horrors of slavery. Their bitterness was against the Portuguese.

I couldn't understand how it is that black women cried and said that it was the Portuguese who had snatched them from the bosom of Africa to sell them, and still they slept with them. There were black women who lived with them as husband and wife. And they had several children and they were obliged to work as domestic servants, and the money they received, they had to give to them. In short, they were their concubines and indirect slaves.

For me, men's lives were like spider webs. I don't know where they get these threads to make their webs. And I don't know where it is that men come up with so many complications to make their lives difficult.

I didn't want to grow up, the lives of grown-ups are disagreeable. I got upset when Mama said that I was growing.

I was already resigned: blacks didn't have the possibility of living in beautiful houses with window panes and yards. My mother said to me, "My dear, it's silly to aspire to what we can't get, we will be able to be happy living in an egg shell."

How I would like to live on a paved street with electric lights. But the streets that were paved, lit up, were for the rich. The light of the poor was little kerosene lamps and coal stoves.

And my relatives drank *pinga* and got drunk. They fought, broke the furniture. What a trial it is for someone who doesn't drink to remain in the midst of drunks! I used to cry because I wanted to be free of that environment.

---

5. The law that abolished slavery in Brazil. It was signed by Princess Isabel on May 13, 1888.

Siá Maruca didn't work. Grandpa wouldn't permit it. He said, "After a woman gets married, she should only take care of household chores. It is the man's place to be the head of the house. I'm earning fifteen thousand réis a week."

What a fortune! He bought foodstuffs in sacks. I was well-fed, I couldn't stand chicken. Siá Maruca used to shout, "Children!" and the chickens would come running to eat the corn. I said, "What peace!," and I was happy.

One day Siá Maruca washed clothes for someone and earned a thousand réis. When Grandpa came home to eat lunch, there was no manioc flour. He didn't eat without manioc flour because, in the time of slavery, blacks had to eat *angu* stew and manioc flour.[6] In the evening, when he went to eat dinner, he found manioc flour. He asked Siá Maruca, "Where and how did you get the money to buy this manioc flour?" His eyes flew to Siá Maruca's face, who was biting her lip. Finally, she decided to answer, "I washed Dona Faustina's clothes, she paid me and I bought five kilos of manioc flour, I washed two dozen pieces of clothing for a thousand réis. Each kilo of manioc flour cost two hundred réis."

My grandfather took his belt off his waist and hit her. He said, "That's the last time you're going shopping without my consent. When you want to go out, ask me for permission. I am the one who controls you! If you don't know how to obey—leave!" Siá Maruca cried.

And I kept thinking, "It's better to be a whore, she sings, goes to dances, travels, smiles. She can kiss men. She wears silk dresses, she can cut her hair, wear makeup, ride in taxis, and she doesn't have to obey anyone."

Grandpa told us that the blacks who lived in big cities already knew how to read and even had money in the bank. He didn't know how to read, but he always tried to find out if blacks were rising in the social sphere. "Oh!," we exclaimed, amazed.

I don't know if it was jealousy, but I noticed differences in the ways Mama treated us. My brother was the favorite. I thought, "She treats him with a lot of tenderness because he's mulatto. And I'm dark-skinned." My mother smiled, saying that mothers like all their children. That a mother fights for one hundred children and the children don't fight for the mothers.

---

6. In some regions in Brazil, coarsely ground, toasted manioc flour is sprinkled on many dishes as a condiment.

She worked in family houses and in whore houses, and she brought me with her. I witnessed those pornographic scenes of women with men. The kisses and the embraces. Then, they would go into the rooms and I would hear those noises of the wire beds. I thought, "If I could only see what they're doing!"

"I adore you! I adore you!"

"Don't leave me, my darling!"

They were the only things that reached my ears. But it didn't satisfy me. Because what I wanted was to see.

The only delicious thing that exists is rice pudding, caramel, and peanut brittle. Cheese-bread. Could it be that a man is more delicious than sweets? To sleep with a man it's necessary to be a grown woman, and I'm little.

Emerenciana was already sleeping with men and wearing silk dresses, and she had had a gold tooth put in her mouth and had changed her name. She was Vilma. She bought a silk dress for her mother, who was happy because her daughter was earning a pile of money, one hundred thousand réis a week. She earned more than a *doutor*. She had already been to Uberaba, Araxá and Uberabinha. And the men, defeated, said "I wish I had been born a woman!"

Men are never going to sleep with me. Because I'm not going to grow up. My mother said that children didn't understand those scenes of kisses and hugs. Oh, blessed naiveté! Children understand a few little things. All of the girls had boyfriends. At the dances, they danced. I was left alone. The boys didn't dance with me, they said that I was very ugly, very skinny. That, dancing with me, they felt like they were dancing with a piece of bamboo. The only one who danced with me was Domingos, a little black boy of fifteen. He had only one arm. I became resentful and that complex was taking over my mind.

My brother fought with me, I was the one who got beaten. And I complained to my mother, "You protect Jerônimo because he's a legitimate child. And me, I'm a bastard." I didn't know what a bastard was. But I thought the word was beautiful. My mother wasn't familiar with it either. We heard it at the circus. Unconsciously, I had hit the mark.

What I disapproved of were the fights of drunken adults. An adult has to have class. Be a good example, be the teacher of decency. And not a teacher of anarchy.

My Uncle Joaquim was the wildest of the family. He was the second to last child, and he made his older siblings obey him. Even my mother, who had raised him after my grandmother's death, had to ask his blessing. He didn't know how to read. He used violence. And he hit with so much energy that the people who he beat either obeyed him or disappeared from the city.

He was living with my baptismal godmother. She was white. And the people murmured, "Where did you ever see that, a black man with a white woman?" And the white men cursed, "It's sugar in coffee. It's coffee with milk. It's a fly in the milk. I don't approve of this union. Birds of a feather should flock together."

The black women, when they saw my uncle strolling arm in arm with my godmother, said, "Look at the fly in the milk! Look at the fly in the milk!"

My uncle said that it was ignorant men who were racists.

One Sunday, my mother made up her face—powder, blush, and lipstick. And she went out for a stroll. She ran into my uncle, who made her go home and wash her face, "It's not *Carnaval*." She obeyed him in silence. When he left, she swore, "I regret having raised that whelp!"

He only respected Grandpa. When he asked for his blessing, he took off his hat and kissed his hands. He was the only one who didn't drink alcohol, who didn't hang out. The police didn't know him. He was a teamster, he made my brother guide the oxen. But, he didn't like to get up at five o'clock in the morning. He would wake him up with his stentorian voice. My brother begged, "Mama! Tell him I have an ear ache. My bed is so nice and warm."

"He can't go. He has an ear ache."

He broke down the door. He entered with a switch in his hand, and he gave us lashes, shouting furiously, "You're sick? Here's the cure! I don't like lazy men, little whelp! Either you learn to work or I'll kill you! Brazil shouldn't be a country of loafers. Our lands need hands. Men are just like that, when you invite them to work, they make up these illnesses: bronchitis, sinusitis, lazyitis." He gave my brother a few lashes. On the third lash, my brother jumped out the window, pulling the blankets after him and crying.

My mother complained, "You're neither my father nor my husband." He gave her a lash and she shut up. I laughed. He gave me a lash saying, "This is so that you'll respect me. I'm not a clown for you to laugh at."

When he went away, my mother would get up, open the door, walk around the house to see if he was hidden, listening to us. Verifying his absence, she swore at him, "That dog! I used to clean his a—"

And my brother decided to get up when he heard my uncle's footsteps. On Saturdays, he paid him. He exchanged the money for change, and filled my brother's hands, and said, "He's very lazy. I pay him with change to motivate him to work. Who knows if the money doesn't carry more weight than my words and my whippings."

My brother put the coins in his pockets and smiled saying, "I'm rich! I'm rich!"

I was envious and thought, "Why is it that I wasn't born a man to get rich and earn a lot of money?"

My uncle used to say, "In order for a man to earn a lot of money, he must be a hard worker and earn the money honestly." I repeated in my head, "Honestly."

My uncle bought foodstuffs, bacon, meat, and *cachaça*,[7] and he said to my godmother, "Make lunch, then you can drink your *pinga*."

She drank the *pinga*. She got drunk, and let the dogs eat the meat and the bacon. She didn't make the meals. The black women said, "Well done! You got yourself a white woman! White women are no good!"

My uncle beat my godmother, who was very drunk and passed out on the floor. It looked like he was beating a corpse. But who dared interfere? When she sobered up, she had a broken arm. She began to whine and cry.

And I thought, "There are women who say men are good. What goodness can a man have if he kills and beats, cruelly? When I grow up I don't want a man. I prefer to live alone."

She fixed up the injured arm. Then continued kissing my uncle.

Those episodes, for me, were an enigma. And I said to myself, "Good Lord. They have no shame." I was naïve, unfamiliar with sexual attraction, which is what governed couples. But my age didn't make me think that my uncle was right.

Those who felt pity went to tell the police that my uncle had beaten my godmother. When the police came, she defended him, "He's a saint! He's the best man in the world. He's not going to jail. I already have the right place to keep him."

---

7. Another name for *pinga,* a strong alcoholic drink made from fermented honey or sugar cane.

My uncle said, "I leave in the morning to go to work, when I come home I find her drunk, fallen on top of her arm. If her arm is broken, I'm not the one who's responsible."

My uncle showed his calloused hands that were the only proof of manhood. The police apologized to my uncle and left. They shut the door and went to bed.

My uncle bought furniture, she burned it to cook the meals. I never saw my godmother wash clothes. She knew how to crochet very well, she wanted to teach me but I didn't learn to follow the threads, I gave up.

She was married to a black man named Alcides. He abandoned her. She didn't have children because she didn't have a normal menstrual cycle, she only got her period twice a year. She was a yellow woman. An indefinite color. When she smiled, she looked like a skeleton.

I heard and saw these disturbances that were stored in my mind as if they were clothes folded up in a dresser. Every day there were things to enter into my head. The human body should be just like that, I thought.

But my uncle got tired of living with my godmother, who was so detached from life, very different from my mother who imitated the bees and the ants who run around from one place to another.

I noticed that he wanted to renew the family. Seeing the difficulty, he disappeared from Sacramento, which is a city that doesn't offer a promising future to her children. My brother rejoiced. He said, "I don't have to work! I don't have to get up early!" And he got up at eleven o'clock and went to warm himself in the sun.

I thought, "My God, blacks need to be dynamic, more hard-working, to make brick houses. And not to become comfortable in these little rooms covered with thatch." Even though my uncle was brutish, I missed him. He was an honest man.

8

The City

This is what happened on Saturdays and Sundays. The city was flooded with men, cruising in search of whores. The whores became agitated, just like termites on rainy days. They said that Saturday was the day to earn a lot of money. They bathed and put on perfume and went out into the streets in search of men with money.

What tremendous contention! They all wanted to get men. They weren't selective. They seemed like copulating animals. A very clean woman slept with a dirty man and kissed that mouth full of rotten teeth. If the man showed money, bang! And he heard this: "My darling! My love! My sweetheart! My little saint!" In exchange for these words, the men gave them fabulous sums. And they gave the money to the mistresses of the boarding houses where they lived.

And watch out when they didn't get any money! What confusion! The mistress of the boarding house swore at her, "Harlot, wretch! You're old now. No one wants you! Go beg for money! You'd better get me the money, or else get out of the room."

I thought, "Could money be that important? But Grandpa says that God is the most important thing there is!"

I thought it was strange to see the whores wearing colorful clothing and exaggerating their make-up and adornments to attract men. In my opinion, they should have cleaned out their mouths so they wouldn't have bad breath. I think that whoever trades her body should be meticulously clean.

On Saturdays, the police got tough. They put a cartridge belt on over their tunic. It was proof of absolute authority. The blacks were panic-stricken. The black women went out, they went to the taverns to get their sons and their husbands. How horrible it is to have to tolerate a crude, imbecilic, arbitrary, ignorant, indecent, and even worse, illiterate, authority. They didn't know the law, they only knew how to arrest people. When they couldn't win the affection of the whores, they arrested the wretches. The whores refused the soldiers, insinuating that they didn't have any money. And that's how I found out that men who have no money have no value for women.

The whores were the ones who wore lambskin jackets and silk dresses. They cut their hair, and put on red lipstick. Married women and virgin girls weren't allowed to wear lipstick, put on rouge, and cut their hair. But when the whores went by with their sensational clothes, the men got ecstatic as if they were admiring something supernatural. And the girls were jealous and wanted to grow up to be whores and sleep with José Merendengo. What a handsome man! He was the Rudolph Valentino of Sacramento.

The whores felt immense pleasure when the men got upset fighting over them. These quarrels were enough to awaken their vanity, convincing them that they were beautiful. What fear they had of getting old! They bought anti-wrinkle cosmetics and were always in front of the mirror. As if they were Cinderella's stepmother. What was not right was the interference of the police with those wretches. They wanted to be the favorites.

The most beautiful loose woman was Abadia. One day she turned up dead with a young man named Octávio.

Octávio had killed her and committed suicide. They didn't investigate it. I discovered who had killed Abadia and Octávio. But I couldn't say who it was. If I told, he could kill me and kill my mother. I was five years old and I already understood the childishness of adults who sometimes act like big children.

I went in any place. And I witnessed all kinds of things . . . I thought, "Grown-ups don't respect little ones." I couldn't understand all of that chaos in detail.

The whores didn't know how to read. They paid someone to write letters for them to send to their relatives.

The traveling whore was a goddess in those circles, telling her friends about the places she knew. They always had money. They sent it to their relatives. They asked that their mothers take care of their sisters, that it was horrible to be a worthless woman, that they make the sisters get married, that it's much better to belong to one man than to belong to all men. That they had many men, but they didn't have a man. On Saturdays, they went out into the streets looking for a man. When they didn't get one, they said that they were unhappy. Could it be that grown-ups are crazy? Could it be that I'll be just like the grown-ups when I grow up? I was already sick of living in this world. I went to ask my mother, "You know, Mama, I don't like this world. Would you put me back where I was?" She explained that, to leave this world, it was necessary to die, "Oh! I'm afraid of dying."

When someone stole something, the military policemen went out into the streets of the city with the prisoner. He was forced to take along what he had stolen: a chicken, horses. And the children ran along behind, banging on cans, frying pans, drums, whoever knew how to play the accordion, violin, guitar, *cavaquinho*,[1] harmonica, went along behind the prisoner.

One day it was a black man. And we yelled, "Look at Joe Blanket! He stole a blanket! Look at Joe Blanket, he's a blanket thief." It was June. How cold it was. But the black man was soaking, as if he had taken a bath.

The people went out into the streets to see the thief. It was as if he were accompanied by a procession. When the chief of police released the prisoner, he disappeared and never again returned to Sacramento. It was a moral punishment that had its good effect. And no one wanted to be a thief. I loved these little celebrations. And the comments, "A man who steals should be branded with a T on his face. A thief has no value. He's a vulture who's too lazy to work, a thief won't last long." Even the children scorned the thief when they got together and commented, smiling, "Did you see how Joe Blanket was sweating?" and they laughed. A man who stole a chicken would lose his real name, he would be known by all as Joe Chicken.

And the years went by. What worried me was the blacks' unhappiness. When a crime was committed or a robbery, blacks were the suspects. The police arrested them. How many times did I hear the

---

1. A small, guitar-like instrument.

higher-ups saying, "Thieving niggers, low-life niggers." They said, "It wasn't us." I noticed their sad looks.

I knew I was black because of the white children. When they fought with me they said, "Little nigger, stinking little nigger!" My mother's grandmother said, "They are like thorns, they grow with the plants." I didn't understand, but I found all this so confusing!

Because the white children criticized our hair—"Straw hair! Stiff hair!"—I struggled to make my hair grow. It was a useless struggle. Blacks are the children of monkeys. How I felt like throwing rocks.

My pleasure was to have a white girl beg me, "Bitita, throw a rock at that mango for me." I was a good shot, I simply threw it and got it. I thought, "Even though I'm black, I have some usefulness."

The children didn't mess with the old blacks because they said that they knew a man who turned into a werewolf and a headless mule.[2] It was the only way the old blacks could manage to have some peace.

The thatch of our house was already rotten. What a struggle for my mother to get together the twenty thousand réis to buy a cartload of thatch and pay a man to put it on our little hut. Whites built their houses with permanent tile roofs.

I became sad. The world will always be like this: nigger here, nigger there. And God likes the whites better than the blacks. Whites have houses with tile roofs. If God doesn't like us, why did He create us?

I went looking for my mother, "Can you give me God's address, ma'am?" She was irritable and slapped me. I was horrified, "Could it be that my mother doesn't see the blacks' struggle? Only me!" If she would give me God's address, I would speak to Him. So He would give a world only for the blacks.

She explained to me that the blacks were ignorant. That a man who doesn't know how to read is planted, just like a tree, in one place. "When you turn seven, you're going to go to school. You're going to learn how to read."

How envious I was when I saw Doutor Cunha reading the newspaper, "I'm going to read the newspaper, God willing." And I was happy.

My mother was meticulous. She scoured the counters, she scoured

---

2. *Mula-sem-cabeça*, a monstrous character from Brazilian folklore. According to Câmara Cascudo, the *mula-sem-cabeça* was a woman accused of being the mistress of a priest. As a punishment for her sin, she was condemned to be forever transformed into a headless mule on Thursday nights.

the pans. She took a bath every day. I didn't like to take a bath before going to bed. She said, "If you don't take a bath, the vultures will come to eat you." Sometimes I went to sleep without taking a bath. In the morning, when I saw the vultures circling in the sky, I went running to heat water to wash my feet. Looking at the vultures flying I shouted, "I already washed my feet, Mr. Vulture." And that's how I got used to taking a bath.

What terror I felt at the time of the feasts of St. Benedict with the blacks rushing around. It was the only time that they gave the shopkeepers any profits. There was no educated black to talk to us about slavery, to motivate the race. They lived without worrying about the future. Anything unusual in the city, the whores tried to get involved as if their presence were indispensable. I thanked God when the holiday that left its tragic consequences was over: several pregnant young women. When the city returned to normal, the host of the party was in debt. Some blacks got sick from dancing so much *samba*.[3] What fanaticism for dancing. I thought, "If they had such fanaticism for working, they could even have houses with tile roofs." For me, the people who lived in houses with tile roofs were important. For several days they kept talking about the songs they had improvised. What horrified me was seeing a black person walk five leagues in order to dance. The few times I went with my mother on these treks, I was a wreck.

When the time for planting drew near, you saw nothing but people looking up and commenting, "Can it be that it won't rain?" Every house had an altar with images of the saints. The women washed the images, praying, "I am washing them so that they will send us rain. Can it be that our good God is going to punish us?"

They decorated and washed the crosses. They said that the state of Ceará went seven years without rain. That a lot of people died. I thought, "The crosses that men make are of wood. What power could they have? Can it be that they answer prayers?"

And I asked that it make me turn into a man. I wanted to plant crops. I wanted to be a strong man and buy a Ford. I wanted to be just like José do Patrocínio who helped free the blacks and even bought a Ford. I had seen the Ford in the newspaper. How I longed to ride in it!

I envied the white girls who wore dresses of velvet, linen, organdy, and wore silk stockings on their legs. Silk cost ten thousand réis a

---

3. *Samba* is the most popular Brazilian dance of African origin.

meter. The woman who wore a silk dress strolled vainly through the streets, like a peacock showing its colored feathers.

When I saw that neither St. Benedict, nor the rainbow, nor the crosses made me turn into a man, I resigned myself and accepted it: I would always be a woman. But even semi-accepting, I envied my brother who was a man. And my brother envied me because I was a woman. He said that women's lives are less full of sacrifices. They don't have to get up early to work. A woman makes money lying in bed. I went running to lie down in my mother's bed, thinking of the money that I would make to buy peanut brittle. Later I got up, unmade the bed anxiously, looking for the money.

When my mother saw the unmade bed, she gave me a hard look and asked, "What are you doing, brat?"

"I'm looking for the money, Jerônimo told me that women make money in bed, I lay down and I'm going to see how much I earned. I want to buy treats." She spanked me.

She earned thirty thousand réis a month. She bought boots for my brother. Twelve thousand réis. And sandals for me. Sandals were the shoes of the poor. I was happy. When it was cold, I could wear stockings. When a poor woman wore stockings, the neighbors asked, "Are you sick?" Only rich women could wear stockings. It was chic.

When there was food left over, the whores gave it to the poor who ate rich people's leftovers without checking to see if they were sick or not.

With the difficulties that parents had just to live, because poverty was their miserable lot, some parents, ignorant, made their daughters become whores. Seeking to get rich through their daughters, malnourished young women who were obliged to spend the nights drinking ice-cold drinks or wandering through the streets looking for an admirer. Some got infected with venereal diseases and died at eighteen. They were flowers who didn't find crystal vases in which to display their splendors. Flowers that didn't find the fertilizer of life, which is happiness.

I didn't like that way of life of the poor. You couldn't even call that life, they suffered more than animals. What a struggle to get money in the rural cities.

What helped was the public slaughterhouse that distributed the entrails of the animals. A piece of liver for each child: if in one household there were eight children, each one got his piece. When the distributor asked, "Are you brothers and sisters?" They answered, "No, sir."

"But you have the same flat noses and the same color."

"It's that we're children of Adam and Eve."

They distributed the heads, the kidneys, the feet, the stomachs, and the tongues. What happiness when we ate the liver fillets with rice! It was a banquet. The meat of the head, what bland meat! It has no flavor and it's hard to cook. There was even a saying: common people were the meat of the head. The choice meat was for the rich: five hundred réis and eight hundred réis a kilo.

When rich children got sick, it was a cough. The poor ones were anemic, had rickets from going barefoot.

My mother cooked over a wood fire. We couldn't buy wood, we went searching for it in the brush. Several women got together: Black Maria, Joaquina, and Sad Maria, my mother, and I. We carried a hatchet. What torture to walk through the brush looking for a stick here, another here. When we found a dry stick, what happiness! It was as if we had found a vein of gold. It was such a trek through the brush, from seven in the morning until noon. I liked to go to eat the wild fruits—*jatobá, pitanga, gabiroba, araticum, maracujá,* and *marmelo-de-cachorro.*[4] I didn't like the return trip. My mother made me carry a bundle of wood. I was weak and couldn't stand the weight. But I couldn't complain. I was already beginning to understand that, in order to survive, we have to submit to someone's whims. When it isn't the mother, it's the husband or the boss. What horrible pain in my legs! The weight pressed me down as if it wanted to push my legs into the earth. When I got home and threw down the bundle of wood, what a relief! I would sit down to rest.

I began to notice that there exists the possibility of becoming free from everything that tires or irritates us one day. Because life is a dish to which we should add a measure of patience. My mother smiled happily because firewood was a problem for us.

The only day I hated was Saturday, because of the excitement. If it were only possible to get rid of Saturday! They only talked about the dance all day. My wish was to transform myself into a bird of some kind, even if it were a vulture, and fly away every Saturday to escape from that environment that didn't please me at all. "Give me the iron! Oh! Wait a minute!" I was already even getting sick of the

---

4. These are names of various native fruits.

iron. But, I was a child. The dance for the women was an obsession.
And the comments, "Today so-and-so arrives!"

The men who worked in the countryside spent Saturday night to
Sunday in the city and arranged women to sleep with. Some already
had a specific woman.

Businesses stayed open Sundays and holidays. They sold alcoholic
drinks, and the drunks wandered through the streets doing strange
things. A drunk didn't earn the respect of the population.

In the city there lived a mulatto named João Flaviano. When he got
drunk, he undressed and the children jeered him. The women gave him
a sheet, he wrapped himself up. He looked like a biblical figure in a
seamless tunic.

What impressed me was seeing the northeasterners with their bundles on their backs, with their famished look, as if they were the
inhabitants of other unhuman planets. Dirty and broken. Some played
violins and sang:

In the state of Ceará
For seven years it didn't rain
Whoever was rich left,
Whoever was poor died.

Several people stopped to listen to them and gave money.

Whoever was rich left,
Whoever was poor died.

The poor had no way to leave the state of Ceará. And I am poor!
That means that when suffering knocks at the poor man's door, he
finds a refuge. I pitied those people. The men looked like walking
skeletons. But I was six years old, what could I do to help that
wretched people?

My mother said, "They are Bahians. They are from Rui Barbosa's
land. They leave their land and go wandering around Brazil looking for
work. Because if they stay there, they die of starvation. It doesn't rain
there."

Wow! Then rain is really necessary!

So, that's why Rui Barbosa wanted to prepare a Brazil for Brazilians? Brazil was discovered in 1500, and if it hadn't been so plun-

dered, the men from the north wouldn't live such troubled lives, wandering from one state to another, because Brazil began in the north. What did they do with the underground riches? They were devoured by the insatiable vultures. They were selfish guys who ate the meat and left the bones for the toothless natives. Guys who clothed themselves and left the Brazilians naked. Then Tiradentes noticed it, understood, fought, and died for us. I'm going to ask Grandpa to pray a rosary for Tiradentes. Poor thing, he was hung. And he was right.

My dream was to see a Portuguese, the much-commented man. But the people said that they don't like small towns, that they were in São Paulo and in Rio de Janeiro.

The children who came home from school spoke of Tomás Antônio Gonzaga,[5] whom they killed, of Brother Caneca,[6] whom they killed. If Princess Isabel hadn't left Brazil, she would be dead, too. So, the world is like that? When someone wants to help the poor, the wretched, they kill him. Brazil began to found schools after it became a republic.

Mr. Nogueira said that the Portuguese didn't build a single school in Brazil, that's why Brazil was so backward. That it would take five hundred more years to give the country a new face, collective culture and solidarity. To stimulate patriotic love in the people.

My mother said, "If you grow up like this, worried about the country's problems, you could lose your head, just like Tiradentes."

"Now, Mama, the children who already know how to read told me that on our flag it says *Order and Progress*. That's to remind the Brazilians that the country must always be in order."

Order is the people working honestly, respecting each other.

I felt envious when I saw the children who went to and came home from school. The streets became sad, there were no more children to play with. I asked them, "Want to play?"

"No, I'm going to study. I want to get 100 on my lessons."

---

5. Tomás Antônio Gonzaga (1744-1809), a poet who participated in the uprising called the Inconfidência Mineira in 1789. He was imprisoned and later deported to Mozambique.

6. Brother Joaquim do Amor Divino Rabelo e Caneca (1779-1825), a priest and politician who participated in the Pernambucan Revolution of 1817. After serving four years in prison, he was freed, only to continue his political activism, for which he was eventually sentenced to death by a firing squad.

I went running home, "Mama! Oh, Mama! I want to go to school because the children get one hundred thousand réis for their lessons. I never saw a one hundred thousand réis note."

My mother didn't answer. She had already explained that I had to turn seven.

The northerners who arrived went to live in the Heritage. When it rained, they watched as if it were the most beautiful sight on earth. In those little bundles they carried pans and plates. They built campfires, picked grass to cover their shacks, and slept in hammocks. Even the birds have their nest, and they . . . They are more wretched than the birds.

On Sundays, the inhabitants of the city had to attend religious services. The predominant religions were Catholicism and Spiritualism. The Catholics were the majority. The Spiritualists, the minority. There was discrimination: the poor and the blacks went to six o'clock mass. The rich, married *madames* went to eight o'clock mass. And the young people went to ten o'clock mass, they went with their boyfriends and girlfriends.

The poor people stayed near the church to see the rich women go by, dressed in their very expensive dresses that were made in São Paulo, in the Casa Alemã or at Madame Antonieta's.[7] If, when washing the clothes, the laundresses lost the label from the article they were washing, bang, they were fired. An article of clothing that was made in São Paulo had value. It was proof that the owners were rich and important.

The poor women envied the fur jackets. I understand that the dream of the poor is dreaming, only dreaming. The rich women were very vain. They looked at the poor as if they were intruders in this world, or bothersome objects without value.

I was worried about the question of class. If there were a middle-class family, and if in this family there were a very pretty girl, when a single doctor appeared, he married her. I heard the girls say, "I don't like him. I'm going to marry him because he's a doctor and will be able to give me a comfortable life and bring me into high society."

I was horrified, because a man, be he rich or poor, when he decides to marry it's because he's considering the woman. He deserves to be

---

7. These are the names of two famous haute couture shops in São Paulo.

loved. I think that women who act like that are slaves to vanity.

Many of the women said, "I like so-and-so. But he's poor." Can it be that high society is all that important?

My mother said that the exigencies of life oblige us not to choose poles. Whoever is born at the North Pole, if he can live better at the South Pole, then he should travel to the places where life is more pleasant.

9

My Son-in-Law

A lady who had moved to Sacramento and didn't mention where she was from, was looking for maids and my mother accepted.

She wanted them to clean the house. The windows, the floors. Make desserts, prepare meats, stuff them, stuff chickens, because her son-in-law was going to arrive. She was going to introduce him to the big-wigs. What hustle and bustle! She sent out several invitations. At home she said, "My son-in-law, what a man!"

We wanted to see this phenomenal man, so praised by his mother-in-law, a rare thing.

My mother and Aunt Tereza were the ones preparing the food. Antônia, the *pai preto*'s[1] wife, was the one who ironed the embroidered tablecloths. The house was beautiful.

The lady was very nice in her dealings with the servants. She didn't give orders with the conviction of someone who is paying. She would ask politely, "Tomorrow, my son-in-law is going to arrive. Could you arrive at six o'clock?"

My mother said yes.

She paced the floor, complaining that the hands of the clocks were

---

1. Literally, "black father." According to Câmara Cascudo, the expression "father" (*pai*) means natural chief, a person with indisputable authority. Thus, one could presume that the *pai preto* was an important leader in the community.

lazy and didn't move. "My distinguished son-in-law was made in heaven. He doesn't offend our sensibilities. He's the soul of politeness." Every place she went she only talked about "my son-in-law." "He's the one who supports us. My two sons are studying at a boarding school. He's the one who's paying. It's not only Christ who saves, he's saving me, too."

On the following day, my mother arrived at six o'clock. She was wearing her new dress and "angel-feet" shoes on her feet. At noon, the son-in-law arrived. He took the Cipó trolley to the city. The driver drove the eagerly awaited son-in-law, him and his wife, and their two children. When they got out of the car, the mother-in-law went to greet him. They hugged and kissed. The mother-in-law said, "I feel like I haven't seen you for ages! You're looking so handsome! Thank you so much for the letters. I have received them every eight days. Your letters calm me so much. You are my protector." She kissed her grandchildren. In a minute the news spread, "Have you heard? 'My son-in-law' arrived!"

"Really?"

"But you know something? 'My son-in-law' is black!"

"Black? Good Lord!"

"And could he be as important as they say?"

"She says he's rich."

The guests didn't go to have lunch. You could tell that that lady was crying inside. And the gossip went on, "Just imagine, me sitting at the table with a nigger."

His wife was a white beauty. Black hair and green eyes. The mother-in-law invited her son-in-law to see the house and the yard with its groves of trees. And she asked my mother to leave only six places set at the table and to take away the other plates so her son-in-law wouldn't notice the hostility of the city's important people. She said, "These men from here aren't worthy to touch my son-in-law's hands."

They served lunch. So many beverages! They opened the windows. How hot it was. He said, "You should have told me that you had come to live in this pigsty. What a city! This is a village. Is there a beach here?"

"No, Sir. When you would like to take a bath, you have to go to the shower."

"These cities in the countryside never grow. The inhabitants of these areas don't have any vision, nor any pride. They don't spend anything for the good of the community. They're people with caveman mentalities, who keep their savings in bottles. Ah! I'm going to take you with me. You have to live in Rio. What select people! There is no prejudice there. Who runs this town?"

"It's Seu² Juca. He's the first mayor of this city, and he came from Araxá. You have to meet him. He's an unforgettable guy. He's a *doutor,* but speaks like a hick. Just imagine that when he visited the capital of the state of São Paulo, he was bowled over by that gigantic city's progress. People from other states, when they visited São Paulo, would have their picture taken in the Luz garden wearing woolen clothing and with an open umbrella to show that in São Paulo it rained every day. Or else that there was that drizzle that made the *paulista*³ capital famous.

"Everything was new to him, not believing that the dazzling city was the work of man. His idol was the trolley. What a thrill, traveling in that electric car that took him to every corner. Yes, he was going to buy some trolleys to bring them to Sacramento. And the trolley would take people from Sacramento to Cipó. It would be a good business.

"He spent his afternoons on the trolley. And he kept traveling from Penha to the city, and from the city to Penha. And he fell asleep on the way.

"When he woke up and got off the trolley, he noticed that everybody was looking at him. He was intrigued, worried, thinking, 'Can it be that these people already know that I'm the mayor of Sacramento? Can it be that they know I'm a plantation owner?' With people stopping for him to pass by, he thought, 'Can it be that they wish to honor me? Can it be that they have noticed that I'm important?'

"He continued on his way. When he passed in front of a store window, he saw his image reflected in the glass. He understood the cause of the stares. It's that while he slept, they had switched his hat for a mason's hat, all dirty with lime and cement. He smiled and went to buy another hat. He was wearing clothes *à la palm-beach,*⁴ polished, pointed-toed shoes, a gold watch, and a politician's insignia. He

---

2. A shortened and popular form of *senhor,* which means "mister."
3. The *paulista* capital is the city of São Paulo, the capital of the state of São Paulo. People from the city of São Paulo are called *paulistas,* whereas the inhabitants of the state of São Paulo are known as the *paulistanos.*
4. In the original, Carolina uses the expression "roupa de *palm-beach,*" which has been translated here as *à la palm-beach* in order to reflect her style.

went into a store and bought another hat. At that time, a hat cost forty thousand réis.

"Some time later, the trolleys arrived in Sacramento. Whoever had the courtesy to steal Mayor José Alfonso's hat had gotten a good deal, because, at that time, only a politician made forty thousand réis."[5]

"Is there a secondary school here?" asked "my son-in-law."

"They say they're going to build one. Would you like to visit the city?"

"No, I'm not used to breathing in dust."

In the kitchen, my mother smiled and said, "The black man's nose is an important nose. It's a big shot's nose."

"I just came to see how you're living."

What a polite black man! He was chubby. He talked about the progress in the big cities. That the people are cultured, more generous, and they aren't lazy.

There was a lot of food left over, sweets. We took them home. Three days later, they left. He invited my mother, "Let's go to Rio de Janeiro." My mother refused, saying she was afraid of suffering.

We never learned that lady's name, nor her son-in-law's name. I wanted to hear his name. But, all she said was, "My son-in-law."

She looked at that black man as if she were looking at a jewel. It seemed like she was the one who wanted to be that black man's wife. The messiah who saved her from poverty. Never was a man so adored by a mother-in-law. That lady's admiration was really impressive.

I think the men didn't go to meet him because they felt inferior to "my son-in-law." The mother-in-law didn't work and she lived as if she were a queen. Every month, the son-in-law sent her five contos.

I kept thinking about that good woman who was scorned merely because her son-in-law was black. That means that the black man made her lose the respect of the whites. My mother said that the world is like that. I was furious, "Ah! The world is gonna change with me. I don't like the world as it is." My mother smiled and asked, "What are you gonna do to the world?"

"I don't want any grown-ups in the world. It's the grown-ups who

---

5. When Carolina says that "at that time, only a politician made forty thousand réis" she probably means that only a politician made enough to casually spend forty thousand réis for a hat. Forty thousand réis would be much too little for his actual salary.

are bad. The children play together, for them, color doesn't exist. They don't talk about wars, and they don't build prisons to keep anyone in. I don't like grown-ups. Grown-ups have the nerve to stick a knife in one another. The other day, I got a thorn in my foot and it hurt so much! And if it had been a knife?" Uncle Cirineu was listening to me and said, "This little black girl will go far."

10

Grandfather's Death

Uncle Cirineu told me, "Look, Bitita, you're going to marry my son Ascindínio."

I thought, "I prefer Cirino." But I didn't say anything. I didn't want to hurt Ascindínio, who was happy and said, "You're gonna be my wife!"

He was a calm black man. I thought, "This calm man, as quiet as stagnant waters, doesn't suit me. I want a lightning-man. These men who get up in the morning and just sit around don't suit me."

My dream was to see a rich black man, a landowner, who owned tracts of land with fields and plantations. I had heard that in Bahia there were blacks who were landowners, who planted cacao. How I liked the blacks and pitied them! Some so rich, others so poor. Why is it that the poor pray every day? They said, "Lord . . . take pity on us . . . Lord . . . full of compassion." Who can this God be who is our Father? How I wished to see God and to ask him to fix the world. Rich people didn't talk about God. Only the poor.

On Sundays, the adult cousins got together. Maria Sebastiana, Ana Rosa and my Aunt Claudimira, each one with her boyfriend. What a struggle for them to keep up a conversation. They were illiterate. They only talked about dances.

"It's Manoel, he's a good accordionist."

"And João knows how to play the guitar."

They were the sons of tenant farmers and worked for the Portuguese. Brazil was like a second edition of Portugal. It didn't have its own style.

And on the farms, there were no schools, there was plenty of work. Pulling out stumps, preparing the land for planting. They would leave at night. They weren't allowed to stay in the city on the weekdays.

The only man who said, "I'm not afraid of the police, because if I want to be a military policeman, I'll become one," was Augusto Bicudo, my cousin Dolores's father. One day, he argued with a policeman, and the policeman shot a hole in his ear. Augusto Bicudo put black wax there to hide the bullet hole.

The news spread, and the circus owner went looking for him. "Don't you want to work in my circus? Now you're worth something, because you have a hole in your ear. You'll work with the clown *Pouca-Roupa*.[1] I'll turn you into a great artist. And I'll pay you fifty thousand réis a week. Free and clear. I'll take you to Belo Horizonte, Rio de Janeiro, Recife, São Paulo, and Niterói. You could even get rich. I can advertise, 'Come see the man whose ear was punctured by a policeman's bullet.' "

And the men commented, "Augusto Bicudo has a pierced ear because now it's in style for a man to pierce his ear."

"No. It was a policeman who punctured it."

"Really? With a knife?"

"No! With a bullet."

He got very hurt and went to live in the jungle with the Indians.

On the following Saturday, the prostitutes got dressed up to wait for the farmhands. But, no one showed up, fearing the police would puncture their ears. Even the businessmen protested, and that policeman left the city.

Dolores cried, saying, "What a pity! They punctured my father's ear!"

We were busy with the preparations for the wedding of Maria Maruca, who was Siá Maruca's daughter. I never found out Maria's whole name. What a pretty mulatta. Such a good woman.

Pretty people shouldn't die. Maria loved Aunt Ana's son, João Marcelino. But, Aunt Ana didn't consent to the marriage. She was

---

1. The name means "little clothing."

authoritarian. She was the one who wore the pants. All she needed were whiskers.

Her children had to marry whites. But her mother, who was my great-grandmother, was a black woman with straight hair. She was the daughter of a white man. I have mixed blood, because my maternal grandmother was of mixed race.

João Marcelino and Maria used to meet at the dances. They were always partners. They didn't speak. They only looked at each other. They weren't allowed to speak. Those were the orders of "the dictator," who was the only negative person in our family. Maria, seeing the impossibility of making a home with João, began to forget him. And she started dating a handsome black man.

Sebastião was from Araxá. What pretty eyes! And they got married. João Marcelino didn't attend. He cried, lamenting that he wasn't free. That he was a slave to his mother's whims. He didn't go to the dance because he couldn't be Maria's partner, who for him had the value of a jewel.

He played the guitar and sang a farewell song. Maria wasn't moved by João's songs. He sang:

They say love comes from luck
and luck is for the lucky.
And, as I'm unlucky,
I never want to love again.

It was a chapter of his life that was closed.

Sebastião, Maria's husband, worked in a quarry. A stone came loose and fell on his back. He was sick for several months. They called a doctor who lanced his back and the pus gushed out: five kilos.

I looked at it, horrified. Maria cried. When the pus stopped pouring out, Sebastião died. They were only married for four years. Once more I hated death—poor Maria!

How a pretty woman suffers when she becomes a widow. Even in the cemetery, the men were already winking at her, as she cried desperately. When we left the cemetery, the women went home. But the men accompanied the widow to her house. They said, "Don't cry, Maria. We can get you some money."

Another said, "I'll get you money."

And the men kept lurking around our house as if they were male dogs following bitches. Men who lived in the countryside came to the city when they found out Maria was widowed. Zica, who was the mistress of a whorehouse, went looking for her. "Go to my house, Maria. You're still young. And you're pretty. You'll make me a lot of money. I have houses here in Sacramento, Conquista, and Uberaba, on São Miguel Street."

Maria didn't know how to defend herself, she was extremely polite. They say that a woman is only a widow during the day. And Maria got pregnant. She drank a lot of remedies to have an abortion, and she got tuberculosis. The baby was the child of a black man named José de Paula. When the baby was born, Maria died.

She left a son of her husband's, who was cared for by his godfather, Jerônimo Gervásio. And the little black boy didn't go to school. I pitied the black child. He was handsome. He was Sebastião's son.

Mr. Jerônimo Gervásio sold his little farm to some Japanese: Napoleão and Karachima. And they moved away. And I never saw the black boy again.

Sometimes I thought, "Mothers should die after raising their children." I thought people died of their own free will. When I saw a dead man, I was upset, "What an idiot, to die and go into the earth. He died of laziness, he didn't want work. Could it be that this man didn't feel bad about leaving his wife, his children, his lands, his car? I'm never going to die, because I heard that people who die never come back."

The case that horrified me was seeing a military policeman kill a black man. The policeman said that he was under arrest; he was from the countryside, he ran away. The policeman shot him. The bullet went into his ear. The military policeman who shot him smiled, saying, "What a good aim I have!"

With his foot, he moved the lifeless body of the wretch and said, "He must be Bahian."

And I kept thinking about the Bahians who were forced to leave Bahia because it doesn't rain there, and to be killed by policemen. Does he have a mother? Who is going to cry for him? He didn't fight, didn't curse, didn't drink *pinga*. There was no reason to kill him. When the judge came, he looked at the dead man and ordered that he be buried. And the case was closed.

And what if Grandpa prayed a rosary asking God to make it rain in the North? And God answers Grandpa's prayers. When he prays, it rains, and the northerners don't have to leave the North and come to Sacramento and be killed for no reason. I cried. He deserved my tears.

The military policeman who killed the northerner was white. The judge was white. And I got scared of whites and looked at my black skin. Why is it that whites can kill blacks? Could it be that God gave them the world? I had a very active imagination, but I didn't come to any conclusion about the facts that I witnessed. I was six years old. The only safe place for me to keep the facts was inside my head. My head is a safe. My mind became very clear.

When my Grandpa got sick, I wondered, "And if Grandpa dies? Who's going to pray for rain? Everyone needs the rain, but the only one who prays is Grandpa. The one who should pray for rain is Father Pedro, because he plants crops, too. Can it be that he prays? And Siá Maruca will be left without Grandpa and she'll have to work. She won't have Grandpa anymore to buy food and clothes."

He was getting weaker. The children who lived on the farms went to the city, bringing along their children and wives. And that's how I got to know all of my relatives. Uncle José Benedito had seven children. The oldest ones didn't know how to read.

The doctors gave up on Grandpa. It was a kidney infection. The doctor who treated Grandpa was Dr. José da Cunha. I was filled with pity hearing the moans. I thought, "My God, why does sickness exist? Where does it come from? Can sickness be from God or from the Devil?" Because I heard everything that's bad is from the Devil, how I hated and cursed the Devil! Evil one, cloven foot! Sending a sickness to hurt my Grandpa!

Oh! If only I knew where Hell is, I would go there. And I would ask the Devil to take the sickness away from Grandpa. My gaze swept through space and I thought, "Where could Hell be? If I only knew the place!"

I stopped playing and sat down beside the bed. My grandfather looked at me. Then he closed his eyes. I got worried, staring at his face, his tapered nose. I wanted to be good-looking, just like Grandpa. What a beautiful mouth! He didn't have the flat nose of the Negro race. Grandpa was the descendant of Africans. He was a son of the last shipment of blacks who came on a slave ship. The

Cabinda[2] blacks, the most intelligent and the handsomest.

Grandpa's house was covered with thatch. Who was he to buy tiles! Tiles were inaccessible to us, we saw tiles on the rich people's houses. Every five minutes someone arrived and would ask, "Is Mr. Benedito better?"

"What a good man! He's going to heaven."

They praised him. He never fought with anyone. He was never arrested. Never being arrested was a badge of honor. I thought, "Grandpa came to the world before, and I came after. I want to hear what they say about him in order to know how he lived."

My uncle João went out to buy bread for the people who were keeping watch over Grandpa's deathbed. But if he met up with a group of serenaders, he would go off singing with the merrymakers. He had a poor memory. He was retarded. He'd had meningitis. He was harmless. He was a wretch.

The women neighbors lent the biggest pans they had, because the children and grandchildren had gathered. We, the grandchildren from the city, were attached to Grandpa, we felt badly and suffered seeing him moan. The grandchildren from the countryside watched him without being moved. One day, Grandpa fainted. The children and grandchildren cried. What a confusion of voices!

"My God! Papa died."

"Don't die, Grandpa."

"If you die, it's never gonna rain again. And we're gonna live just like the northeasterners, walking, walking, with those sacks on our backs."

And I hated death and wanted to give it a thrashing. Death is crazy! It comes looking for men who like to work, those who have obligations, who have their children to raise, the orphaned children will be left in the care of Doutor Brand.

---

2. Cabinda is a Portuguese enclave on the western coast of central Africa. The name is geographical and doesn't designate an ethnic group. The main ethnic group of the Kongo River basin is the BaKongo, a branch of the Bantu language group. In the 1780s and 1790s, the Cabinda area was the scene of fierce competition between the French and Portuguese over control of the lucrative slave trade at the estuary of the Kongo River. Aided by reinforcements from Brazil, Portugal managed to gain control of Cabinda by the early nineteenth century. It is highly probable that most slaves who claim Cabinda descent are not actually from Cabinda; rather Cabinda may only have been their point of departure from Africa.

The *doutor* has a young son, Humbertinho, and he does things to the girls. Can it be that the judge's sons don't have to be well-bred, and can do whatever they please? The judge wants us, who are poor, to toe the line. I don't know what line that could be.

I think that the poor children are better bred than the judge's son. Dona Sinhá, the judge's wife, is a very good woman. But, Doutor Brand noticed that his son harasses the poor girls. When they see him, they run away. If I were a man, I would want to give the judge's son a beating.

Rich people raise their children like this, "Don't do that, Humbertinho!"

"Behave, Humbertinho!"

"Go study, Humbertinho!"

But what Doutor Brand's son needed was a good spanking, a good beating, and hard work.

Can it be that Death didn't notice that she disturbed men's lives?

Grandpa fainted from the pain. Later, he recovered and said to us, "I'm not fainting. It's that I'm dying, and whoever is dying remembers the past. I remembered that I owe Mr. José Rezende thirty thousand réis. I bought a roll of wire and didn't pay. You'll pay."

And his gaze went around, looking at his children, and he said, "Joaquim is missing. You could call on Saint Anthony to make him appear."

My mother went to look for Dona Maria Treme-Treme,[3] who said she had supernatural powers and talked to the saints. She asked for a brand new towel, that had not yet been used, a new strainer, and a package of candles. My mother bought them and gave them to her.

Every two days, Grandpa fainted, when he woke up, he would reveal something to us. He said it was good to die when the Ten Commandments of God's law were obeyed. The worst thing, what God doesn't forgive, is stealing and killing your fellow man. I was curious, and wondered, "What could the Ten Commandments be?"

One day, he asked Siá Maruca to sit by his side and listen to him. Whenever he was going to speak, the neighbors, the children, would go to listen to him. The only grandchild who went to listen to him was me. I wanted to stay near him, because he was taking leave of this world. Preparing for his long trip. A trip on which men don't take

---

3. Literally, the name means "tremble-tremble."

suitcases, their luggage is the good acts that they did here on this planet. Those who heard him speak said, "This man is a prophet."

He said to her, "Maruca! You lived in my company for twenty-one years. When a woman lives with a man for seven years, he should marry her. If it wouldn't make you sick to marry a dead man, I'm asking you, would you marry me?"

"Oh!" we exclaimed.

She smiled. "Ever since I came to live with you, my dream was to become your wife. I didn't ask you to marry me because it still isn't common for the woman to ask for the man in marriage."

The children went to look for the priest to marry them. What turmoil, what agitation! Grandpa could die at any minute. Siá Maruca kissed him and caressed his cadaverous hands, "God help you. What would have happened to me if I hadn't met you? I have no one in this world, I'm going to be alone."

"You'll be with God. At weddings, there are parties, dances, the bride wears a veil. But ours is different. Instead of a white dress, you will wear a black dress. They celebrate weddings with parties and a honeymoon. But our wedding will have tears, a few days from now, I'm going to die. What a strange wedding trip, I'll travel alone to the beyond. I don't know if I'll be happy! Because man is born pure, and dies impure."

I thought, "What does that mean, pure and impure?"

Mr. Manoel Soares said that Grandpa was illiterate, that it was his spirit talking through him. I decided to ask what a spirit was. "It's his soul, we all have a soul that guides us."

"And the soul is good?"

"All souls are good."

"Then why is it that the soul doesn't teach men how to be good? They kill each other and don't regret it."

I was thinking about the military policeman, Ovídio, when he killed the northerner. They killed and disappeared, fearing the relatives would take revenge. Mr. Manoel Soares didn't answer.

Grown-ups have the strength to build houses, to cut down trees, but they don't have the strength to be good. Grown-ups are fools.

What impressed us was the letter that Uncle Joaquim sent us from São Paulo. He had been imprisoned in the penitentiary for four years.

My uncles were idiots, and godfather Candinho, who wanted to be the most enlightened of the family, said, "Whoever is in São Paulo is almost in heaven. There is so much work there that if the dead come out of their tombs, they soon find work. Now that I know where brother Joaquim is working, I'm gonna write him so he can get me a job in the penitentiary; then I'll come get the family."

We were happy. In the letter he said that he missed Dad. "But I can't come see him. At night, I hear a voice calling me: Joaquim! Joaquim, go see your father. The voice called me four times. Then, it was silent. But the voice stays inside my brain, it calls me seven times. Could I be going crazy? What's happening there?"

My uncle went to comfort Grandpa, "You don't have to be sad or to worry about brother Joaquim, because he's very well, he's working in the penitentiary in São Paulo."

Grandpa said, "No, my children, he's not well. He committed a crime. He's a convict. He was violent, and violence hurts us. My poor son!"

It was the first time we had heard of the penitentiary. Nobody answered the letter.

They didn't thank Dona Maria Treme-Treme who asked for a brand new towel and a strainer and told us, "Seven days from now you will receive a letter."

Could it be that she talked with the saints? She proved what she had told us. She wasn't pretentious. Nobody sought to learn her art from the woman.

I felt like I was dreaming. One night, Grandpa fainted. My Uncle Antônio got a candle and a crucifix and put them in his hands. I looked at those hands, skin and bones, cadaverous, that used to be strong. That had worked to make the Portuguese rich and worked to raise children and grandchildren. I looked lovingly at those honest hands.

Grandpa opened his eyes and said to us, "Every evil that one does is paid for. Good and evil are sacred debts to God, and we receive everything with interest: good and evil. It's better to forgive than to take revenge. I'm my mother's youngest child, when she was dying, I put a candle and a cross in her hands, and now, Antônio is doing for me what I did for my mother. It's a pity you don't understand."

I wanted Grandpa to explain to me what death was like.

"We're all mortal. Nobody is the master of the world. The world is a hotel where we spend some time. Everything around us is dust. Iron, with time, turns to dust. A piece of furniture will also become dust. Everything in the world is earth."

When Grandpa fell silent or fell asleep, the children had to play far away from the house, so as not to wake him up. The grown-ups didn't talk.

The people who came to visit Grandpa left commenting, "What an intelligent man. If he knew how to read, he would be the African Socrates."

"What could the 'African Socrates' be?"

Others commented, "Not educating him was a crime. This man would be The Man! They could create a general education law, because educated people who acquire knowledge of their intellectual level have the ability to see inside themselves."

Some words kept spinning around in my mind. They were these, "It was a crime not to educate this man." I knew what crime was. When Ovídio, the military policeman, killed the Bahian, I heard several people say, "It was a crime to kill this man." Some words I heard and didn't understand. I smiled and thought it was funny.

Someone, seeing me smile and not seeing the reason for that smile, said, "She's crazy!"

There were times when I said to my mother, "Mama, Mama! Look at the snakes!"

She smiled and said, "I don't see anything, dear!"

I felt like thousands of snakes were coiling around me. And a huge snake was rushing in my direction. I wasn't scared! Grandpa told me, "They're the false friends that you're going to meet in your life."

I didn't understand anything. "Grown-ups make me confused when they talk. And my mother always says that I'm going to grow up. I'm fine as I am. My God! I'm afraid of growing up. Could it be that I'm going to learn all these horrible things that grown-ups do!"

On August 27, 1927, Grandpa died. My mother told me I was six years old. Could I have been born in 1921? Some say that I was born in 1914.

I noticed that the blacks didn't know how to read. I never saw a book in a black person's hands. Blacks didn't serve in the army because they didn't have birth certificates, they weren't drafted. They said, "It's pride. Only whites are considered Brazilians."

Nobody in my family had a birth certificate. A death certificate wasn't necessary to bury the dead. We went back to talking about my distinguished grandfather.

I cried when he died. Can it be that it's still going to rain? Now he can talk to God. He's going to ask for rain for the north, and the northerners won't need to walk, walk to exhaustion. I touched my Grandpa's cold body and thought, "Why did he get cold? It's hot out!"

Grandpa's casket was blue. My aunts cried. Others said, "He's at rest."

At five o'clock, the funeral procession left. The men carried the coffin. The men said, "It's our common end."

Siá Maruca begged, "Mr. Benedito, you're my husband, come for me! I liked life only because you lived. Not everyone learns how to live in the world and I . . . didn't learn."

After the burial, some went out to drink, and my mother cried. As time went by, I began to forget Grandpa, who was the most handsome black man I ever saw in my life. What a beautiful nose! His forehead and mouth were magnificent.

11

School

My mother went to wash clothes at Mr. José Saturnino's house, and his wife, Dona Mariquinha, told my mother to put me in school. My mother went to talk to the teacher. I went with her. When we entered the school, I was scared. On the walls there were some pictures of the human skeleton. The classroom was large and the classes were in the corners. The morning session was dedicated to the fourth grade.

The teacher was Mr. Hamílton Milon, the brother of the founder of Alan Kardec School.[1] It was Mr. Eurípedes Barsanulfo who founded the school.

The second period was for the first, second, and third grades.

When I looked at the pictures of the skeletons, my heart beat faster. Tomorrow I'm not coming back here. I don't need to learn how to read. It's that I was offended by my classmates for having said, when I entered, "What an ugly little black girl!" No one wants to be ugly. "What big eyes, she looks like a frog."

My mother was poor. Dona Maria Leite insisted that Mama send me to school. I only went to see what school was.

---

1. Carolina uses the spelling "Alan," but she means Alain Kardec (1804–1869), the French Spiritualist thinker and the founder of Kardecism, a Spiritualist movement. Spiritualism is a religion based on the belief that the dead continue on as spirits. These spirits help the living, who communicate with them by means of a medium.

Dona Maria Leite lived in Chapadão Station. She visited the city of Sacramento twice a year to attend the Spiritualist session in commemoration of Mr. Eurípedes Barsanulfo's birthday. She gave clothes to the poor children, the clothes and books were new, to motivate us and make us feel proud. If the rich children went with new clothes, the poor did too. And there were no complexes.

What I appreciated is that Dona Maria Leite didn't help the whites, only the blacks, and she said to us, "I'm French. Your odyssey isn't my fault; but I'm very rich, I help you because I feel sorry for you. Let's educate you to see what it is that you show us: if you are going to be sociable and, having knowledge, will be able to avoid delinquency and follow righteousness."

To make us proud she said, "I like blacks. I would like to be black and I would like to have a very flat nose." And she smiled. The little black children who already knew how to read would read for her to hear. She listened with great interest.

My mother was shy. And she said that blacks should obey whites, that is, when the whites were wise. That's why she should send me to school, so as not to offend Dona Maria Leite.

When I went to school, I was still nursing. When I felt like nursing, I began to cry, "I want to leave. I want to nurse." My late teacher, Dona Lonita Solvina, asked me, "So, you still nurse, little lady?"

"I like to nurse." The students laughed.

"So, little lady, you're not embarrassed to nurse?"

"No!"

"You're getting to be a young lady, you have to learn to read and write and you're not going to have any time to nurse because you need to prepare your lessons. I like to be obeyed. Are you listening to me, Dona Carolina Maria de Jesus!"

I became furious and responded insolently, "My name is Bitita."

"Your name is Carolina Maria de Jesus."

It was the first time that I had heard my name, "I don't want this name, I'm going to exchange it for another."

The teacher slapped my legs with a ruler, I stopped crying. When I got home, nursing made me sick. It's that my teacher knew how to convince me that I should stop nursing. I understood that I still nursed because I was naïve, and school enlightened me a little. My mother smiled, saying, "Thank God! I struggled to wean this brat and I couldn't manage to." My mother felt she had benefited from the first day of class.

My Aunt Claudimira said, "It's because you're silly, if this little black girl were my daughter!" My mother smiled, commenting, "Thank God! I'm free! Now I can go out."

I heard all that without understanding. I felt like I was dreaming.

I kept going to school. Because attendance was obligatory. But I wasn't interested in my studies. My teacher insisted that I learn how to read. She gave me a tender look. I thought learning to read was very hard.

I begged my mother not to let me go to school, "I don't want to learn to read."

She heard me and gave me two lashes. I went against my will. I was lazy. When I missed class, the teacher sent a student to look for me at home. When I arrived at school, Dona Lonita said, "You are so intelligent, try to learn to read. Exert your mind."

The only letter that I learned to write easily was "O," and in my notebooks I wrote only the letter "O" and I said, "The little wheel is easier."

Seeing that I wasn't interested in my studies, she drew on the blackboard a man with a trident in his hands who was stabbing a child and she said to me, "Dona Carolina, this man is the inspector. Any child who doesn't learn how to read by the end of the year, he sticks with his pitchfork. At the end of the year he's coming here and I am going to introduce you to him and ask him to do something with you because you don't want to study. He's probably going to stick you with his pitchfork."

That picture impressed me deeply. I looked at the picture, and I looked at the book. I dreamed about the drawing and screamed, "Mama! Look out for the inspector! Send the inspector away because I swear that I'll study. I'm going to learn to read. Don't let him stick me with the pitchfork."

Mama said, "Sleep, girl, you're delirious."

I decided to study diligently, understanding that we should even thank someone when they want to teach us. I understood that I was being disrespectful of Dona Lonita, trying her patience.

The drawing stayed on the blackboard, three months. Later, I noticed that I now knew how to read. How good! I felt great inner happiness. I read the names of the shops! "Armond Goulart's Brazilian

House." It's not just this shop that's a Brazilian house. But the houses, the trees, the men who are born here, everything belongs to Brazil. I noticed that those who know how to read have a better chance of understanding. If they get off track in life, they will be able to readjust. I read, "Model Pharmacy." I went running home. I went in like a ray of sunshine.

Mama was startled. She asked me, "What's this? Are you going crazy?"

"Oh! Mama! Now I know how to read! How good it is to know how to read!"

I rummaged through the drawers looking for something to read. There were no books in our house. It was a poor house. Books enrich the spirit. A neighbor lent me a book, the novel *Isaura, The Slave Girl*.[2] I, who was already fed up with hearing about the tragedy of slavery, decided that I should read everything that mentioned what slavery was. I understood the novel so well that I cried out of pity for the slave girl. I analyzed the book. I understood that, at that time, the slave owners were ignorant because whoever is educated doesn't enslave, and those who are educated don't accept the yoke of slavery.

It was a time of *tête-à-tête*[3] because an educated person foresees the consequences of his actions. The whites, upon taking the blacks out of Africa, didn't foresee that they were going to create racism in the world, which is a problem and a dilemma. I read the book, got the meaning. And thus, my interest in books increased. I never again stopped reading.

I became one of the best students in the class. The class was integrated. My teacher said at the end of class, "I want to talk to my black students, it's a very important matter." The whites left and we stayed. She said, "I am noticing that my white students are more studious than my black students. The whites don't make mistakes when they write. They wash their hands when they are going to touch the books. Their drawings, what works of art! They excel and get 100 every day."

Now I understand what getting 100 means. It's when the lesson is done well. When we left school, we were furious and thinking: the

---

2. *Isaura, The Slave Girl (A Escrava Isaura)*, written by Bernardo Guimarães (1825–1884) in 1875, is the classic Brazilian antislavery novel, often compared to Harriet Beecher Stowe's *Uncle Tom's Cabin*.
3. In the original, Carolina uses the French.

white students . . . they're not going to know more than us!

After a few days later, she asked the white students to stay after class. She told them that the black students were the most diligent, the most studious, the most able in their schoolwork. "They're going to be promoted and you white students are going to fail. You're going look ridiculous because everyone thinks that whites are more intelligent than blacks. I'm delighted with the progress of my black students."

The white students left the class indignant. Each one commenting, "Just imagine a black wanting to be better than me. I, who am white, have to be the best. These blacks are going to pay!"

Acting in this way, she had no problems with the homework.

She lent us books to read at home, *Sacred History, General History,* the Bible, and the books were passed from one to another.

12

The Farm

One day a man appeared in the city. He said that he was looking for a woman to live with him on a farm. That it wasn't possible for a man to live in the country alone. He asked if my mother wanted to live with him. She accepted.

He said that the proper place for the poor was in the countryside. That country life, besides being healthier, is simpler. City life was difficult because we had to buy everything.

He went to find a farmer who would hire him as a tenant farmer. We were going to live on the Lajeado farm, near Uberaba.

The owner was Mr. Olímpio Rodrigues de Araújo.

It was with a heavy heart that I left school. I cried because I wouldn't receive my diploma for two more years. My only choice was to resign myself because the parental decision always wins.

My mother boxed up our kitchen utensils, I boxed up my books, the only things I venerated.

The one who drove us to Lajeado farm was the driver, José Fernandes. It was the first time I had traveled by truck. It was able to go so fast!

When we arrived, I was unhappy, I wanted to return to the city. I looked around that place, seeing only the trees with their shades of light and dark green.

Mr. Olímpio Rodrigues de Araújo paid the driver two hundred thousand réis. My mother cried, "It will be so long before we can repay this debt! . . ."

My step-father, Mr. José Romualdo, encouraged her, "God will help us. This year we will suffer a little. But next year, it will get better. This year we are going to plant crops."

I kept thinking, "Can it be that we'll be able to live in the brush?" I was afraid of going hungry. "This here, it's very sad. It has no appeal." My mother caressed me and told me, "I was born in the country. And I was raised in the country. It was the only period in my life in which I was happy. I still miss the time when I was a girl. You, when you were younger, didn't want to grow up. I didn't want to either. No one wants to grow up, but everyone grows up."

I already knew that the laws of nature are unchangeable. I ran my eyes all around. Only trees and a blue sky with a tepid solar disk. My mother continued, "I began to suffer after I went to live in the city, it was in the city that I learned to like vices, the city thrills us, and it destroys us. I had no time to be at your side, I went to work away from home, and you were left wandering in the streets. Here we will be friends."

A few days later, I began to appreciate the quiet life of the country. Saturday was quiet without those dances. Dona Maria, Mr. Ilarêncio's wife, gave us milk and cheese. The people who visited us gave us a pair of chickens as a gift, "It's for you to get started."

My mother got out of bed as soon as the sovereign star began rising, she would prepare our meal for us to go work in the fields. I stayed in bed, listening to the birds singing. When Mama insisted, I got out of bed, I went to wash up in the spring, staring at the water that sprang from the bosom of the lead-colored rocks and was always tepid. The breeze wafted softly. I breathed in the perfumes that the wild flowers gave off.

The farmer gave us three *alquileres* of land to plant. We planted rice, beans, corn, sugar cane, and sorghum. There was still land left. How good it is to have land to plant! I was already understanding the value of the land that knows how to compensate man's efforts. And the earth's womb is fertile. The earth is female, it's the mother of humanity. I was getting used to that green world.

When the harvest came, I was astonished at the earth's prodigality. A friend who every month offers us something to harvest. We planted two bags of rice, we harvested thirty. Two sacks of corn. We harvested three cartloads. My step-father made a storehouse. What plenty. The chickens multiplied, only black and white spotted ones.

If the earth didn't act like that, there would be no incentive for man to do the rudimentary work. I began acquiring the habit of planting, becoming semi-ambitious. I was the first to get out of bed to go to the fields.

In my free time, I read Henrique Dias,[1] Luis Gama, the martyr of Independence, our Tiradentes. All contemporary Brazilians, and those of the future should pay homage to the late José Joaquim da Silva Xavier.[2] He wasn't a bandit, he wasn't a pirate, he was one of those who also dreamed of preparing a Brazil for Brazilians. By reading, I was acquiring solid knowledge.

We began to raise pigs. We intended to buy a cow, but it cost 120 thousand réis. My mother said, "You dream too big."

What a delicious life! I was amazed by the plenty. Vegetables and fruits, for me all that was the land promised to Moses that I had the luck of finding.

On Sundays, we went visiting at the house of the first tenant farmer, the richest, Mr. Florêncio. He had 20 cows, pigs, and more land to plant. He was the farmer's marriage godson. He was a seventy-year-old man and he asked for the farmer's blessing to flatter him, "Your blessing, godfather Olímpio." Mr. Olímpio Rodrigues de Araújo didn't answer. If a baby boy were born, bang!, his name was Olímpio.

I was very much in love with our new life. I was forgetting about buying kilos of rice, and becoming used to the 100 kilogram bags and to the storehouse. Everyone had the chance to make sweets. My mother made rice pudding with pure milk. I ate it. She asked, "Do you want more?" That "Do you want more?" kept resounding in my brain. We were given the milk, the sugar. We planted the rice. What peace, the police weren't on our heels. What silence for sleeping!

We planted twenty-two *jiló*[3] plants. Every Saturday, my mother collected forty liters, I would sell them in Uberaba. I sold each liter for

---

1. Henrique Dias (?–1662), fought against the Dutch in Brazil from 1637 to 1638. He also fought to get rid of the *quilombos,* communities formed by runaway slaves.

2. Tirandentes's real name.

3. *Jiló* is the fruit of the *jiloeiro* plant and belongs to the Solanaceae family, which includes tomatoes and eggplant. It has a bitter taste, but is widely cultivated in Brazil for food by the poor.

300 réis. I earned thirty thousand réis, I bought dresses and a blanket of pure wool for twelve thousand réis.

Every week, a foreign family arrived to live in Brazil and said, "What a country! What *buena tierra*. What *buona terra*. Long live the Brazil of the Brazilians!"

The Italians said to their children, "Three years from now we'll be rich." And the children worked, singing the music of Verdi, they were happy because they were going to be rich. Even the illiterate blacks sang *La donna è móbile*.

The only black families who lived on Mr. Olímpio Rodrigues de Araújo's farm were: Mr. Romualdo and Antônio Cavaco, who was widowed. And my step-father wanted me to marry him.

When a tenant-farmer got sick, he would go to the farm to ask the farmer to call a doctor. What a struggle! The farmer said, "Give her some orange leaf tea."

"I already did!"

"Give her some *erva-cidreira*[4] tea."

"I already did!"

"For the doctor to come here, he'll charge a lot."

And the doctor didn't come.

When the sick person died, the farmer said, "Oh! If I had known that she was really sick, I would have called a doctor."

I thought that it was laziness. When we went to visit the farmer's house, I was disappointed. It wasn't as I imagined. It had no furniture, only some rustic benches, a table, some pallets with mattresses of straw. I thought, "They are the owners of this huge piece of land, they should be happy." When I saw the farmer's daughter, I felt sorry for her. She was an idiot, deaf and dumb. She threw her food on the ground and ate it mixed with mud and feces. Poor little mistress ... She was so pretty! The other son, Zezé, was a semi-idiot. He went to boarding school at Pedro II School in Rio and didn't learn to read.

They were the offspring of a consanguine marriage, a marriage between cousins to keep the wealth in the family. The farmer's wife lamented, they were unhappy. I thought that it was only the poor who were unhappy. The farmer's wife, Dona Maria Cândida, was very skinny, as if she were the descendant of a snake. She was too simple, she wore slippers; she wore round, full skirts. There was so much cloth

4. *Erva cidreira* is a mint-flavored herb believed to have medicinal value.

that they must have weighed about three kilos. The jackets full of frills were to give more volume to her body. When there's no possibility of filling out the body with one's own meat, it must be filled out with cotton.

She spoke with my mother, asking her what she knew how to do. My mother responded politely. My mother was of the Free Womb,[5] and she said that it's the whites who are the masters of the world. She learned to say to the whites only, "Yes, ma'am; yes, sir."

When it was my turn, the farmer's wife examined me closely with her gaze. As if I were for sale, saying that I was a clever little black girl. She envied my mother who had a perfect daughter. Her envy multiplied when she was told that I knew how to read. She asked my name. My mother answered with a quavering voice, because the presence of a white person terrified her, "Her . . . name is Carolina Maria de Jesus."

I asked my mother to tell her that my name was Bitita. The farmer's wife told me that her oldest daughter's name was Carolina, "You're namesakes." My mother smiled and told me, "You have your grandmother's name."

I didn't like my name, thinking that this name would upset my life. My mother had already said that we can't change our names. It's forbidden.

Dona Maria Cândida asked my mother if I could come every morning to help her to clean the house. My mother agreed. I thought, "How great! I wonder how much she's going to pay me?"

But Dona Maria Cândida told me, "You know, Carolina, you come work for me, and when I go to Uberaba, I'll buy you a new dress, I'll buy medicine to turn you white, and I'll get another medicine to straighten your hair. After that, I'll get a doctor to narrow your nose."

I thought, "So, these men who work here used to be black, and the farmer's wife made them turn white! And when I have straight hair and a narrow nose, I want to go to Sacramento so that my relatives can see me. Can it be that I'm going to be pretty?"

I went to work for Dona Maria Cândida for six months. I got up at five o'clock, washed my face quickly because I intended to always

---

5. The Free Womb Law, signed by Princess Isabel in 1871, was a first step in the abolition of slavery in Brazil. According to this law, the womb of the slave was "free," which meant that the children born to slaves were free.

arrive on time so as not to upset her. She was the most important woman to me.

I rejoiced inside when she told me that she was going to Uberaba. I anxiously awaited her return.

She was gone for two days. When she returned, she found me on duty waiting for her, but I was disappointed. She didn't bring any packages. So, she had tricked me! I thought of the six months I worked for her without receiving a penny. My mother told me that it was not yet possible for blacks to lodge a complaint. I cried.

I looked at my black hands, caressed my flat nose and my straw hair, and decided to remain as I was born. I didn't ask Dona Maria Cândida for anything, she's the one who used a trick to cheat me. I couldn't and I shouldn't call her names, she was powerful. We depended on her to live, she gave us land to plant. But I silently cursed her! I understood that she was already paying with her idiot children. Only two were healthy, Toninho and Carolina: Tuca.

The next day, I didn't go wash clothes, and she didn't call me. My mother smiled and said, "If it were only possible for me to explain so many things! But time is also a teacher and it will teach you. Those who learn for themselves learn better."

We worked on the farm for four years. After that, the farmer kicked us off his lands. "Go away, I don't want you on my farm. You don't bring me any profit. You only give me debts, your harvest is poor."

My step-father asked, "If you would lend me the plow to till the soil, sir."

"I'm not giving you anything, go away. You go sell vegetables in Uberaba, you earn a lot of money, and you don't share it with me."

He sold a thousand sacks of quality coffee, *moca*[6] coffee. He sold a hundred fat pigs to the freezers, and we earned thirty thousand réis from the vegetables and he wanted a share.

On these farms it's only the farmer who was the right to earn money, "You owe me eight hundred thousand réis and you don't repay me. I'm not your father."

My step-father got daring and told him, "I don't want to be your son either. Because your children are born idiots. Even the animals are born with a little intelligence, and your children?"

---

6. A superior quality of coffee coming originally from Arabia.

The farmer went in, he shut the door saying, "Oh, if only the punishment stake[7] still existed!"

I thought about the debt that he said we owed, if my step-father never asked for a penny. They didn't give money to the tenant-farmers.

I cried with a heavy heart to leave our little house, the vegetables, the *jiló* plants. Mr. Olímpio Rodrigues de Araújo was the only man who knew how to read. We offered a driver our pigs and the fowl and he brought us back to Sacramento.

---

7. A reference to the stake where disobedient slaves were tied and whipped as punishment.

13

I Return to the City

I thought it was terrible to have to buy a kilo of rice, a kilo of beans.
Why is it that we couldn't have land to plant, and we couldn't buy it?
In the city, life among those people who didn't respect each other was
horrible. And there were fights every day, with the interference of
policemen who beat the ruffians. Those people didn't change their
habits, which were working, drinking, and dancing. How I missed the
merry life of the country! I remember when Mama roasted flour. The
water driving the flour-mill. When we made bread, with twenty eggs
so it would be soft. Everything was prepared with milk. I missed my
hoe. I missed the calluses on my hands. The horse, Maçarico. I wasn't
worried about tomorrow. I wasn't nervous because I lived with plenty
at home.

In the countryside there was no entertainment, but there was no
suffering. But why dream if the lands weren't ours? My step-father
was sad because that daily commotion bothered us. Our house was
full of comings and goings. My cousins, their friends, and other
intruders.

We found work on the small farm of the Japanese man, Napoleão,
weeding rice. I earned three thousand réis, my step-father, five thousand réis. We received it on Saturdays. We would buy ten kilos of
rice and beans. We endured that life. My mother washed clothes for
the rich.

To my unhappiness, my legs became covered with sores. I cooked herbs with which to wash my legs, and the sores didn't heal. I got scared when the harvest ended. With my legs covered with sores, I couldn't work as a domestic. And living dependent on my step-father and on my mother was an agony for me.

One day, there appeared a black man looking for employees to work in the coffee harvest in the state of São Paulo. Mr. Romualdo accepted. We got together eight people because we were going to harvest coffee. Several people were necessary.

We embarked on a Monday. At Restinga station, a cart was waiting for us. It was 11 o'clock when we arrived at Santa Cruz farm. The owner was Mr. Oliveira Dias, Loló. We slept on the ground like animals because our things were at the station. In the morning, my step-father went to pick them up.

The administrator was a mulatto, José Benedito. He gave us a house to live in. There were only electric lights in the farmer's house. In front of his house, there was a cross lit up with electric lights. It was at the high point of Restinga station, the cross could be seen at night.

We were not allowed to plant. The farmer gave us a note worth 150 thousand réis so that we could shop in a store over in Restinga. We had to walk four hours to go shopping, the money wasn't enough. We bought beans, lard, flour, and salt. We didn't drink coffee because we had no sugar. There was no soap to wash the bedclothes. What powerlessness!

Work we had in excess, food, very little. At the end of the year, he held a dance in a house that they said was the old farm house. He bought beer. He gave old clothes to the farmhands. Even used toothbrushes. I kept looking and thinking, "This is an injustice."

My step-father was sad, all of the farmhands were sad. After lunch, Loló went to ride around the farm and see if the farmhands were working, and he counted them, "One is missing, why didn't he come to work?"

"He's sick."

"Here on my farm, getting sick is prohibited."

Riding a black horse and biting his nails, he looked at us, complaining that our work was unproductive. In his presence, we harvested faster. When he left, we sat down because we were weak.

In the farmyard there were vegetables, dairy cows. He sold these things to the farmhands. When someone went looking for him to settle accounts, he said, "You owe me." If we asked for a draw, he chastised us, "I only see you eat, I don't see any work."

Dolores, my cousin, got work in Franca. My sores healed, I went to work in the city. A domestic servant. And I was happy. My step-father ran away, we went to fetch my mother and Adãozinho, the son of my aunt who had died of *barriga d'água*. It was because of suffering a lot on the farms that I wrote a poem: "The Farmhand and the Farmer."

The poor, having no means of living in the city, could only live in the country to be exploited. That's why I say that the suppliers of residents for the slums are the rich and the farmers. If they allowed us to plant beans and rice in among the coffee plants, I would even return to the country. The earth where coffee is planted is fertile, it's fertilized. The beans are full grained, and the rice, too.

I don't like today's farmers. I liked the farmers from 1910 to 1930. Who encouraged the poor to plant. They didn't kick the farmhand off their lands.

Today they do this: they give land to the farmhands to plant; when harvest-time grows near, the farmer kicks the farmhand off the land and keeps the crops and doesn't pay the farmhand anything.

The farmer has a justification, "The land is mine, I pay the taxes. I am protected by the law."

He's a legal thief. And the farmhand comes to the city. Here he is transformed. A simple man no longer knows how to work the land. He knows how to work in industry, that's now weakening. And the farms are, too.

Now, there's a minority to work the land, and a majority to consume. But the little people struggled a lot to see if they could manage to live from agriculture. They are blameless. The country that has the most land on the globe is Brazil, therefore, our people should already be settled.

14

The Domestic

We left everything we owned on Loló's farm when we ran away. We got to the farm poor, and we left poorer still. We tended twelve thousand coffee plants, and we harvested, too, and we got nothing for it. What cruelty! To take us away from our home, to exploit us, and to abandon us without a penny.

In the city we had nowhere to live. My mother went to live in the little room of Mariinha, who was upset, saying that she couldn't entertain her lover. My mother cursed me as if I were responsible for that tragedy. The only thing I did was curse Loló. The only revenge at my disposition. My books were left on the farm.

How hungry we were! We got together fifteen thousand réis and we rented a little room in the house of an Italian couple. For two days we lived in peace. But, on the third day, the rent money ran out because the landlord spent it on alcohol. He began cursing us, "Go away, lazy niggers. Get out of my room."

They wanted to rent the room again to get money to drink *pinga*. They were then dominated by alcohol and didn't respect the thirty days of the month.

Dolores got a boyfriend, she went to live with him, she took my mother, who said that employers act like that with employees.

I managed to get a job with Mr. Benjamim, a Syrian who had a shop in the countryside, he didn't know how to read, he sold by eye and earned money. His wife was also illiterate. When they sold something on credit, she took a pencil and scribbled on a piece of paper, which was for the customers to see that she had written it down. They never added up the daily receipts, they kept no records, they paid no taxes. They were stealing from the country.

My work was to cook, wash clothes, and iron. They promised that they would pay me forty thousand réis. I worked for two months. I became disgusted with them when I saw them fighting with their goddaughter, Nilza, and her husband, a teacher. The Syrian didn't like the teacher, he said that he was Brazilian and poor. But it's in Brazil that they're getting rich.

I asked to settle my account. They gave me five thousand réis, they should have given me eighty. I had to travel by foot to the city. I cursed the Syrian, Benjamim, and his wife, Dona Maria. Money-grubbers.

When I arrived in the city, my mother was working for Mr. Higino Calleiros's brother. They were good to her. Sometimes I would help her with the cleaning. One day, I went to clean behind a cabinet, I threw hot water behind it. I filled up a twenty-liter can with pure cockroaches. They were horrified, so was I.

We managed to rent a house from Dona Narcisa. Fifty thousand réis per month.

What a tragedy the farmer, Loló, caused us! What mustn't the wretches who had stayed on his farm be suffering! If we got together money to pay the rent, we didn't get money to buy food.

My mother decided to return to Sacramento, there she had her little house. We returned. She struggled to get something to eat. My legs were healed over.

I went to work in Mr. Armand Goulart's house. I wasn't up to the work, I left and stayed at home. It was hard to get a little money, I went to work in the pharmacist, Manoel Magalhães's house. They were happy because they were hosting their nephew, Father Geraldo. They considered themselves important because they had a priest in the family. He arrived from Rome, he was going to say a mass. Everyone was invited.

I wasn't familiar with the house. I stayed only in the kitchen and the yard, when there was an uproar inside. I only heard the words, "It's gone! It's gone! It must have been her." I was hanging clothes on the line when I saw two military policemen arrive, "Come on, come on, you tramp. Thief. Disgusting woman. Leper."

I was startled, "What happened?"

"You even ask that straight-faced! You stole one hundred thousand réis from Father Geraldo."

It was ten o'clock in the morning. The news spread, "Bitita stole one hundred thousand réis from Father Geraldo Magalhães."

"Good Lord! She's going to hell!"

They went to tell my mother. She's the only person who is always present in our happinesses and our misfortunes. "Did you steal it, Bitita?"

"No, ma'am! I never saw a hundred thousand réis."

My desire was to see bills of one hundred, two hundred, five hundred, and that of a conto of réis. I was only familiar with bills of fifty, twenty, ten, five, two, and one thousand réis.

I was arrested by two military policemen and a sergeant. I thought, "Can it be that they're going to make me run through the streets, with the children shouting, 'Bitita, she stole one hundred thousand réis.— Bitita stole one hundred thousand réis!' "

I understood that all blacks should expect this.

When the military policeman was about to beat me, the telephone rang. The priest said that he had found the money in his cigarette case. He wanted to apologize to me.

The family wouldn't permit it, saying that blacks have the minds of animals. The proof is evident, they only know how to dance and drink *pinga*. The priest said that he would pray, to ask that God help me in life.

My mother said, "How wretched you are." It's that I was sick.

My Aunt Adriana said, "If Bitita gets better, she's going to be rich! She's very intelligent. But, she won't get well."

My mother said, "When you were little, you were so intelligent, after you grew up, you got stupid."

I drank tea made of *"carolinha velame"* herbs, did everything they told me.

A man arrived looking for a maid to work on Doutor Wanderley Andrade's São Gabriel farm in Conquista. The laundress would earn fifty thousand réis a month. The cook, seventy. My mother decided that we should go, they would pay for the transportation.

What a farm! I was crazy about land. I envied those who had lands to plant. I understand that those who like it don't have it. But my dream was, "I'm not going to die without getting a plot of land for myself. I intend to plant lots of groves of trees."

The mistress was Dona Elza. Very pretty. She chose me to be the cook and my mother to be the laundress.

They made butter. What plenty! Milk, cheese, and meat. I ate to get my strength back.

The mistress was going to travel to São Paulo. I was going to take care of her children at her mother's house. We would go to a farm near Delta station. My mother would stay, taking care of the farmer's house with another maid. The mistress would buy two bottles of medicine for me to take to heal my legs. We prepared for the trip, she took leave of her relatives. They were all farmers.

We stopped at José Rezende's farm. I had to wash the children's clothes, tell them stories, care for them. Not let them hurt themselves. We arrived at Dona Bárbara's farm.

Her son-in-law is the one who took care of the business, Nhonhô. They were going to pack clothing for the girls, Elza and Zenaide, who was chubby, who were going to study at a boarding school in Uberaba, a school run by nuns. I thought, "When they come back from school, they will be arrogant, pretentious, choosing people to offer their smiles to." They have the chance to divide up the world. Money puts the poor on one side, and the rich on the other.

I took care of the two boys, Oswaldo and Gabriel. I said to Gabriel, "I'm going to get a little black boy to play with you." He answered nervously, "A black boy no, a black girl."

Dona Elza had bought a pressure-cooker. When we went to cook the beans, the air didn't go through the place that whistled, the pressure-cooker rose up into the air, fell into the pigsty, rolling around from one side to the other. If it touched a pig, it burned it, the pig squealed, and there was a lot of confusion. It's that I was pretentious, I said I knew how to cook with that pan. It was the first time I'd seen such a pan. I understood that a pretentious person can cause a disaster. How I hated my humiliating condition!

One day I went to look for roots to make tea. But there were so many snakes that I got scared. I jumped in terror of stepping on the snakes.

Mr. Nhonhô got on his horse and went to see what was happening. I couldn't explain that I had come to look for roots, he chastised me, I returned home and went to take a bath, I was sweating.

Dona Bárbara was raising three black orphan girls, their mother had died, their father had given her the girls, who were now learning how to cook, wash clothes, and iron. They had raised a deaf white girl who ironed clothes and made sweets. It was an old black northern woman who cooked. She cried because of a toothache. The only tooth in her mouth. She didn't like me because I knew how to read. Whoever knows how to read can be decent or no good.

In the cold season, how I pitied the farmhands' children with those thin clothes, trembling with cold. And the boss's children with woolen clothes, purchased in São Paulo. The poor children were the stronger ones, they felt nothing.

The mistress traveled for a month, São Paulo, Rio de Janeiro, Santos, and Campinas. When she returned, what a dinner! She wore a fur coat, hat, and gloves. They told her that I was crazy.

When we got back to Conquista, she fired me. She gave one hundred thousand réis in payment, for me and for my mother. She said that she would pay me seventy cruzeiros. I should have received two hundred twenty-one thousand réis. And my mother, one hundred fifty.

We had to go on foot. She gave us a check. I cashed it in the city, I bought myself a dress, another for my mother, and we traveled.

I thought, "They exploit us, but they are going to spend what they gain on medicine." My mother said, "You know how to read, and they make a fool of you."

When I wanted to curse the boss, Mr. Wanderley de Andrade, my mother didn't permit it, saying that he could kill us or send the employees to beat us up. I thought, "It's the right time to quit working for farmers." How I hated them. We arrived in Sacramento. We had no money to buy food. I swore, "I prefer to beg rather than to work for farmers."

15

Illness

I heard that in Uberaba there were good doctors. I decided to go there on foot. I got my bundle and left. I didn't say good-bye to anyone.

I slept by the roads. I walked along the roads. What a struggle!

When I arrived in Uberaba, I didn't know anyone. But, I remembered that I knew a black woman who lived there. How envious I felt when she received me. They were living in a house with a tile roof. It's only me who will never have the possibility of living in a house like that.

She received me coldly. She was Dona Maria Leonaldo. A greeting without a smile, without the customary, "How are you?" She had a goiter, she told me that she was going to have surgery. I told her that I had only come to Uberaba to see if I could manage to cure my legs.

She said that they were very well, that her daughters went to dances every Saturday, that they had good jobs. Her daughter, Londinha, was separated from her husband, Juca, but, as they had no children, Londinha's life didn't change. At night, her daughters began arriving. They didn't greet me, they just looked me over and wrinkled their noses.

At Dona Maria Leonaldo's house there slept a lady, a brown woman. She was the cook for a rich family. At night, she would bring coffee, sugar, soap, and she gave it to Dona Maria. I figured out that she was stealing from the mistress. It was very hard to get on Dona

Maria's good side. Dona Maria told me that the only place available for me to sleep was in the chicken coop. For one who had already slept by the roadside, anything would do.

I spent the night in the yard, it wasn't possible to sleep with the birds. What a long night! I even came to miss the sun's warmth. At six o'clock, Dona Maria's daughters left for work. I was envious. At eight o'clock, she opened the door and said that she didn't want me in her house. That if I could get work in a wealthy house to help with the rent payments, she would then tolerate me, "But, no one's going to hire you. You can go to the St. Vincent de Paul shelter, there, above the Abbey, the sisters will accept you. It's a place for the indigent. It's best that you go right now. The houses that bear St. Vincent's name can't refuse hospitality to those who ask for it."

I got my bundle and left. They pointed the shelter out to me. When I arrived, I went to talk with Sister Augusta. I told her my misfortunes. I then felt like ending my life, "I'm poor, and besides being poor, sick. Hidden sicknesses don't stop us from working, but visible sicknesses do."

I was already tired of living on the fringes of life. "You should have faith in Christ. He's testing your composure, if you have patience. Why think about dying if we all have to die one day."

The sister invited me, "Come in. You are the guest of St. Vincent de Paul." She rang the bell. The sisters appeared. She introduced me, "This young woman is our guest. Your name is . . ."

"Carolina Maria de Jesus."

"You are not the only one who is 'of Jesus,' we all are. He is our Savior."

I raised my eyes and saw a crucifix. I looked at Christ on the cross and thought, "It's horrible to be poor! How did Christ have the courage to be born in poverty! He had no home. And neither do I."

They showed me to my room. In the little rooms, that were divided, there were three beds in each. I looked at the little old women who were now taking leave of life.

At three o'clock, we went to have coffee. What plenty! How much bread!

Sister Custódia told me that the doctor visited the shelter every eight days. That I was to wait.

At six o'clock, they served dinner. Good food. And I thought, "The people of Uberaba are superior, they don't leave their indigents abandoned." In Sacramento, there wasn't even a Santa Casa.[1] In Uberaba the streets were already paved. The city was large, there was no lack of work.

The next day, I asked Sister Augusta, who was the mother superior, for permission to go for a checkup at the Santa Casa. She let me go. The doctor who examined me gave me some medicine, "free samples." When I would take a medicine, I thought: if only it's possible for me to wake up tomorrow well.

The sisters said that I should wash the other patients' clothes.

I washed the clothes of the thirty people who were sheltered there. My legs didn't heal.

I got tired of that life, I told Sister Augusta that I wanted to go back to my hometown. There was no adequate treatment.

She implored me, "Don't go! The world is a theater of sorrows."

I couldn't go to the hospital because I had to wash the clothes. In order to go to the hospital, I had to wait in line to receive a voucher.

The patients shouldn't have to work. But the sisters couldn't get laundresses. It made them nauseous to wash the patients' clothes. I couldn't decide. To win me over, I was given the right to eat the sisters' food. What food! What purée! It was almost a special deference.

But I wanted to get well. How envious I felt of Geralda, a little black woman who was the shelter's cook. When I wandered through the streets, I only looked at the black women's legs.

Sister Augusta's words kept turning around in my mind, "The world is a theater of sorrows." And the scenes are awful: robberies, people killing each other. And the fights with family members. And sometimes with neighbors, "God doesn't want to make you healthy in order to free you from getting too deeply mixed up in worldly concerns. Especially those like you, who haven't yet received adequate instruction, you don't know how to protect yourselves from the false pleasures of life. Moral ruin is also harmful."

I was already becoming familiar with the bitter part of life. But my desire was to be able to give my help to my mother. I think that it's the duty of children to help their progenitors.

The sister gave me some books for me to read, the life of Saint

---

1. A Santa Casa is a charity hospital associated with the Catholic Church and run by nuns that provides free medical care to indigent patients.

Teresa, of Saint Anthony. I am going to fight to get well, I will yet see my relatives envious of me. I will not always remain like this, classified as human garbage. I apologized to Sister Augusta, and left the shelter. I had no money to pay my passage. I went on foot. I walked for four days, I slept under the trees. I asked for food at some houses. But I didn't want to take advantage of my illness.

Several people advised me, "You don't know what you're missing. With these sores you could be rich. Making a lot of money."

"Really?" I wanted to know how I could get rich if I didn't see any possibility.

"Look, go begging. Travel. Go be a beggar in São Paulo or in Rio, there are lots of tourists there, you could even live in luxury hotels. During the day, you beg for alms, at night, you're a personality. Are you familiar with *God Bless You*[2] by Joraci [*sic*] Camargo? You can even lend money for interest."

"I'm ashamed! My desire is to give alms. And not ask for them."

I don't approve of those who commercialize their illnesses. Along the roads, some gave me food, others gave me cheeses. The *mineiros*[3] don't have a lot of money to pass out like you pass out compliments.

How envious I felt of the young women who passed by with their arms around their boyfriends. It's only me who has no one. How I would like to have a good, tender man to live by my side. I don't want a drunk. They are irrational. I want a cultured man. I breathed a sigh of relief when I arrived home.

"Are you healed?"

"No, ma'am."

"You should have stayed there until you healed."

But how could I heal if I washed clothes from five to five? I began to miss the shelter. Even the well from which I drew water to wash the clothes. But I didn't drink that water. A woman had committed suicide, she threw herself into the well, that was now three years ago.

My cousins didn't greet me when they saw me. I thought, "God will help me. One day I will leave this city never to return again."

---

2. *God Bless You (Deus lhe pague)*, is a play written by Joracy Camargo (1898-1973). It tells the story of a man who gets rich from begging.

3. People from the state of Minas Gerais.

16

The Revolution

One day dawned confused, with the streets full of soldiers. It was the revolution. I was only familiar with the ants' revolution, when they move from one place to another. But the revolution of men is tragic. It's men killing one another.

And the people only spoke of Getúlio Vargas[1] and João Pessoa.[2] It was the union of the state of Paraíba with Rio Grande do Sul. The lieutenants yelled at the men to get into uniform. The men shouldn't be left out at the hour in which the country was in dispute. "These seditions happen because of the ignorant people and despots who want to govern the Nation. With Getúlio, we are going to have more jobs. He is the founder of the Workers' Party."

The soldiers circulated through the streets, some carrying green, yellow, and white flags, with Getúlio's portrait in the middle. Those

---

1. Getúlio Dornelles Vargas (1883–1954), took power in a coup-d'état in 1930; he was then made president in 1934 and held power until 1945. He instituted many social programs to win popular support. He was re-elected in 1950, and killed himself in 1954 in the midst of a scandal claiming that Vargas's staff members tried to assassinate an Opposition politician.

2. João Pessoa Cavalcanti de Albuquerque (1878–1930), was a politician and the vice-presidential candidate of the Liberal Alliance (*Aliança Liberal*) in 1929. His assassination in 1930 contributed to the outbreak of the Revolution of 1930, which resulted in Vargas taking power in Brazil.

who looked at the portrait sympathized with him and said, "Now Brazil is going to be in the care of a Man! This is going to give the country a push. We are a people without a leader. We have to wake up. The country can't continue lying down eternally in a splendid cradle.[3] Our country is very backward."

The young women who were domestic servants didn't leave their bosses' houses. I was working in Dona Mimi's house, the Gaúcho's[4] wife. He was happy because it was his state that was putting Brazil in order.

I walked through the streets. At that time, I was using a cream that had a horrible smell, and the soldiers didn't mess with me. My sores were my safe-conduct. I heard the soldiers singing!

Long live our revolution!
Brazil is going to rise just like a balloon.
With Getúlio, Brazil is going,
with Getúlio, Brazil won't fall.
We're going to have more bread on the table,
Getúlio is the friend of the poor.

The rei denomination, the thousand réis, was collected. A note called the *bônus* was put into circulation. The men in uniform received a quantity of *bônus* to leave for their families. Those who received the *bônus* bought food for their relatives in huge quantities. Those who were used to buying kilos, bought sacks. What plenty! The women said, "If Brazil were always like this, this would be a paradise."

Some bought construction materials, others bed linens. Many young men joined up. Those who became involved with the revolutionaries traveled as soon as they put on the uniform.

For those who had an idea of what it is to observe carefully, it could be seen that that revolution was being prepared for some three years. They didn't make mistakes, in each unit there was a truck that carried the uniforms, boots, woolen overcoats. And what a lot of meat!

There was no looting. It was prohibited in the countryside. The violators punished. Those who didn't join up didn't get the *bônus*.

---

3. The phrase "deitado eternamente em berço esplêndido," translated here as "lying down eternally in a splendid cradle," is a direct quote from the Brazilian national anthem.

4. *Gaúcho* is a term referring to a person from the state of Rio Grande do Sul.

My brother didn't want to join up, he said that he was afraid of the revolution. Senile men joined up in order to get the *bônus*. They bought material to build a little house. They said, "If I die, I'll leave this house for my children." For the poor, that revolution was a time of plenty.[5]

My brother wanted to see the soldiers. He decided to dress as a woman. He put on one of my sister's dresses, he put on a necklace, put on make-up, tied a scarf around his head, and went out. A half-hour later he came running into the house. He got undressed, washed his face, put on his own clothes.

Some soldiers came by and asked, "Didn't you see a pretty mulatta around here?"

My mother answered, "I didn't see one, no, sir."

They were looking for my brother. He looked pretty wearing the women's clothes. The soldiers withdrew saying, "What a pretty mulatta! I never saw anything like her! Can it be that she's already married? Pretty women get a man quickly. I just wanted to look at her because we can't bother the women. The revolution doesn't permit it and punishes us."

My brother trembled. When the soldiers left, he disappeared.

The people were confused. They had voted for Mr. Júlio Prestes[6] and were waiting for him to take office. At that time there were rivalries between Minas and São Paulo. The people said that the revolution favored the man from the country who could leave country life and live in the cities, finding work in the factories. Factory work didn't require skilled workers.

And soon, the hoes were disdained and the plows became inactive. Brazil would stop being an agricultural country in order to transform itself into an industrialized country. The people said that Getúlio Vargas was giving loans to those who intended to start industries. It was the first time in the history of Brazil that a president gave incentives to the people, raising their morale. The poor people said, "Getúlio will be our guiding lantern."

---

5. In the Portuguese, Carolina says that it was a time of *vacas gordas,* "fat cows." This expression is a Biblical reference to the story of Pharaoh's dream of the seven fat cows, symbolizing seven years of plenty, who were devoured by seven thin cows, years of want. Gen. 41:1–4.

6. Júlio Prestes de Albuquerque (1882–1946), was governor of São Paulo from 1927 to 1930, and was elected president of Brazil in 1930. He never took office because of the Revolution of 1930.

When Brazil stabilized, those who had received the *bônus* went to exchange them at the tax collector's office. They turned in the *bônus* and received the thousand réis that, at the time, were the catch-all. It was "value-received" money, it wasn't the official currency.[7] The "value-received" money was prevalent. When someone had one hundred thousand réis in his pocket, he felt like he was almost a banker. He was a peaceful man because he had no financial problems.

Those who received the thousand réis when they exchanged their *bônus* said, "It's true, Getúlio is really a man of his word! The man isn't kidding around. The man is really serious."

And acting like that, Getúlio is going to prevail. Those poor young men, who got into uniform and entered the state of São Paulo, never went back to their own states again. They got jobs in São Paulo. In their correspondence with their relatives, they began convincing their relatives to move there. And that letter passed from hand to hand, convincing us that the state of São Paulo is the paradise of the poor. And I thought, "When I recover my health, I want to get to know the city of São Paulo. I want to see the city that's a branch of heaven."

And the men, when they got together, talked about Getúlio. Who was the father of the poor. And I began to like Getúlio, and I thought, "Can this be the politician who's going to prepare a Brazil for Brazilians?" He had reanimated the people, that apathetic people, "leave it for tomorrow," were dreaming, imagining, and planning, because they could trust in the government that didn't disappoint them.

Those who designed projects said, "I'm going to São Paulo and I'm going to get a loan from Getúlio and open an industry with fifty workers, because Getúlio said that if the worker is employed, he won't have time to go astray and become marginalized. He only gives loans with the goal that the beneficiary will be the worker. And industry in São Paulo gives immediate profits."

When the farmers were left alone, they left their lands and moved to São Paulo. The old people said, "One day they are going to regret it

---

7. The Portuguese expression "dinheiro valor-recibido," translated here as " 'value-received' money," rather than being an actual economic term, is a phrase Carolina uses to describe how the thousand réis was used after the revolution. Although it was no longer the official currency, it was used as such, and thus received its value from the way in which it was used.

because agriculture also helps the country. Now that the man from the country is going to the city, there will be fewer productive laborers. There will be a minority to produce for a majority to consume. In the end, the consequences will be disastrous because man works iron, but he doesn't eat iron."

I thought, "Why can it be that, in the small cities you don't feel the effect of a policy? If they are making so much progress in the capitals, they could do it in the country, and a man wouldn't have to move from one state to another." But my city continued the same as ever. I looked at the city and thought, "Poor Sacramento, it's like a cake into which they didn't put any leavening, it doesn't grow."

Mr. Manoel Nogueira said, "Now Brazil is going to stop being a backward country. Revolutions always help the country. The people should have had a revolt to put Rui Barbosa into the Catete."[8]

Those explanations of Mr. Manoel Nogueira's didn't enthuse me any more. When I was a girl, I thought that everything he said would come true. Now I understood that governments come and governments go, but the poor always stay poor. The dreams of better days were not for us. We lived like Saint Laurence[9] on the fiery grate.

What made us even poorer were our ramblings on the farms. I noticed that the farmer doesn't give the farmhands money. In my opinion, slavery had merely diminished a little bit. It was horrible to see the farmhands going around with torn, mended clothes, as if they were beggars. Could it be that the revolution would help the man from the country? Help or sorrow? In a few days the people only said, "Getúlio! Getúlio!" Even the children. What faith! What confidence the people put in the government that's going to take office! As if it were a balm for their difficulties.

My brother didn't want to join up. But a man who didn't fight wasn't a man. Fighting for Getúlio, it's as if he were depositing money in a bank. And the interest is going to be the well-being of our people.

---

8. The Catete, or Palácio do Catete, was like the White House when Rio de Janeiro was the capital of Brazil. After Brasília became the capital in 1960, the Catete was turned into a museum.

9. A reference to Saint Laurence of Rome. *The Book of Saints* describes him as one of the most celebrated of the martyrs of Rome. In 238, Saint Laurence was imprisoned and held for a few days while they tried to get him to give up Church treasures. He was tortured and, in the end, roasted alive on a gridiron when it was discovered that everything had been shared among the poor.

Those who were mounting that revolution were the rich. But why did they revolt? Those who should have revolted and who should revolt are we, who are the poor, who work without improving our quality of life, we only earn amounts that don't cover our needs. We have to stay semi-literate because higher education is only within reach of the powerful.

They say that it's in the big cities that the poor will be able to raise themselves up a little. Longevity for the poor can only be had in the state of São Paulo, where the poor have the possibility of eating every day. And the second state is Rio Grande do Sul. The big industries are in São Paulo because of the quick profits. The men from other states would put their factories in São Paulo. But the countryside continued apathetic.

Thank God that I was alone, I managed to find work in Mr. Manoel Soares's house. What a struggle! Washing, cooking, ironing for the whole family. I worked so as to have a place to eat.

I thought, "If I had lands to plant, I would be rich." I looked at those lands all around the city, uncultivated, the lands were Mr. Hermógenes's, Jerônimo Cardoso's, and João Borges's. Why don't they give these lands over for the poor people to plant? There would be plenty for them and for the poor. It's clear that the lands have to have their owner, but they could rent them out for an indefinite period. Rui Barbosa, who was a stentorian voice in the country, said that lands should be ceded to those who wished to cultivate them, and he wasn't heeded. The last resort is to look for other, more promising, corners. And men are losing the habit of planting. The Japanese man, Napoleão, had stopped planting rice, he had to pay the farmhands. In Europe there was a rumor that the Brazilian black, because of having been a slave, worked for free in exchange for *pinga* and food.

17

The Rules of Hospitality

My mother gave me thirty thousand réis and I thought, "With this money I'm going to Ribeirão Preto to see if I can manage to be admitted into a hospital. Who knows if this time, with God's help, I'll manage to get well."

They said, "Either you're unlucky or they've put a hex on you."

How I felt like laughing because I don't believe in hexes. I didn't say good-bye to anyone. The ticket cost twenty thousand réis. In order to succeed in life, it's necessary to think and act. I arrived in Ribeirão at six o'clock in the afternoon. I paid six thousand réis for a place to sleep, and I asked the doorman to wake me up at six o'clock.

I didn't sleep thinking, "Can it be that I'll be happy here in this city?" How afraid I was of big cities! And I had money.

I got up, got my bundle, and left. I went along Saudade Avenue. I arrived at the Santa Casa and asked for an appointment. They treated and bandaged up my sores and said that I should come back in three days. It was an out-patient sickness.

Where to stay? I remembered that Aunt Ana lived in that city, and I decided to ask around to find her. I managed to locate her. She lived in Vila Tibério. When I arrived it was six o'clock in the evening. They were eating supper.

I stopped in the doorway and greeted her, "Your blessing, Aunt Ana!" She didn't answer me. Even without this invitation, "Come in,"

I went in and sat down. My feet were swollen inside my shoes, which pinched them.

It was Saturday. Aunt Ana said to me, "You certainly have already eaten supper."

"No, ma'am." She gave me a furious look. She put out a little bit of beans and rice while saying, "Eating guests don't interest me. Working guests do. How did you find my house?"

"A woman showed me it."

My Aunt Ana became furious, cursing, "Oh, wicked woman, wretch. May she go to hell!"

I ate and I was still hungry. My cousins were getting dressed. They were going to give a dance, they had rented a dance hall. They decided that I should go because they didn't know me and couldn't leave me in the house alone, "We don't know if she's a thief."

Marcelina was engaged to a little black man named Otávio. I thought, "So now Aunt Ana intermixes with blacks. Her pride is weakening." And I was hopeful that she would help me. How I felt like sleeping!

José Marcelino arrived. He didn't greet me. He looked at me with rancor. I thought, "What a disagreeable character!"

The people who were at the dance were elite. Well-dressed. The men wore cashmere jackets. I thought, "Can they be rich?" At midnight, they raffled off a roast chicken. How I felt like grabbing that chicken and running off. I was sitting near Aunt Ana, watching those who were dancing and thinking, "They're from the other side of the world. The world that health confers on them." For me, that was only a vision. That I could look at. But I couldn't take part. I was now calmer. The treatment that they gave me in the Santa Casa was effective because the sores began to hurt. I couldn't moan at the dance. Sick people don't go to dances.

Next to Aunt Ana was seated a woman who was over fifty years old. She looked at me and asked my aunt, "Who's she?"

My aunt observed me minutely and said, "She's a beggar who comes to my house from time to time asking for alms."

"Poor thing. So young and already unable to face life. How charitable you are!" And Aunt Ana smiled at the woman's praise.

I was tired, but I couldn't even doze off. To end the dance, they decided to dance a quadrille. But there weren't enough ladies. So, they invited my aunt, the other lady, and me.

What torment when I went to get up. My legs were swollen and heavy, as if my feet were made of lead. My wish was to say, "Young man, I can't dance. I'm sick." But he could say to me, "The place for a sick person isn't in a dance hall, it's in a hospital."

I accepted the invitation. He smiled at me. I smiled, too. It had been a long time since I had danced. It wasn't my favorite pastime.

Badly dressed, I was the Cinderella in those surroundings. I was asking God for that quadrille to end. I didn't know if I was paying attention to the music, to the pain I was feeling, or to the steps of the quadrille. The dancers smiled and I felt like moaning. What a relief when the quadrille ended.

The people said good-bye, and we went home. When we arrived, my aunt gave me the hall runners so I could cover the cement and lie down. When I breathed, I smelled the scent of dust. I didn't fall asleep because of the cold. I got up and sat in a chair. I didn't feel sleepy because I was hungry.

When day broke, I got up and went into the yard. Aunt Ana was counting the money she had earned from the *buffet*.[1] They didn't offer me breakfast.

I was so deeply hurt that I didn't feel hungry. At two o'clock, they gave me a few beans. I went out, I went to Bárbara's house, Aunt Ana's daughter. I wanted to see Sebastião, her husband. When she saw me, she shut the door and told me she was on her way out.

I thought, "If some day I'm healthy, I don't want any contact with my relatives, they're showing me their negative qualities." Relatives should have helped and should help one another.

I remembered Sister Augusta, "The world really is a theater of sorrows."

I returned to Aunt Ana's house. I was dirty. Three days without taking a bath in unbearable heat. But they weren't going to let me take a bath in the bathroom. I understood that they were treating me with great disdain so that I would leave the house. I went out to see what I could find in that city.

I met my godfather's wife, Maria Rita. I thought of asking her to stay at her house, but I was now getting afraid of other people's houses. She took in laundry, fine clothes. The yard was large, I

---

1. Carolina uses the French word *buffet,* and it appears in italics in the original.

could construct a little room for myself. I said good-bye.

I arrived at Aunt Ana's house, I spoke with Marcelina, saying that I had visited Maria Rita. "Good Lord! That woman is no good! You shouldn't have gone there."

Aunt Ana said, "Why aren't you going to go out and beg." I was startled. Beg, at my age? It was horrifying. I thought, "I'm going to try! And may it be as God wills." I went out walking, looking at the houses, seeking one at which to beg. Whoever is sick doesn't think about death. "I want to get well so that I can do some kind of work. I'm going to have my own house! God will help me."

Aunt Ana said, "If you don't get any money, don't come back."

Money: it's the key that opens the hearts of the ambitious, "I swear that I'll never sacrifice anyone to get money for myself. I will control my ambition. How can they demand money from a wretched person like me." Oh, my God! When we are born, we cry, and that crying is the foreshadowing of the halo of unhappiness that will crown our brow. All who are born suffer.

I looked at that city. I felt like I was all alone, without God. At last I decided. I rang the bell at a house. A lady appeared, I asked, "Could you please help me, ma'am?"

She looked at me closely, as if I were an object for sale, or on display, "You're very young and you're begging. Aren't you ashamed? That's why no one likes blacks, you're lazy, worthless. Go work, loathsome creature."

"It's that I'm sick."

"Go look for the Santa Casa!"

"They won't admit me. My sickness is out-patient."

"Don't you have a mother, don't you have relatives? You worthless people thank God when these wounds appear on your bodies so that you can take advantage of your illness by begging. It's that you, who are ignorant, don't know the value of a healthy body, without illness."

It's horrible when someone thinks you're disgusting. I went on without saying good-bye, thinking, "I'd rather die of hunger than beg. When can it be that I'll get well?" My dream was to be healthy in order to get money and compete with my cousins. I wanted to transform myself from Cinderella into a princess. My relatives looked at me with disgust on their faces and that hurt me deeply. There were times when I envied my cousins who could buy clothes, dresses of pink silk, blue, and black velvet belts. But black was my fate.

For me, the most beautiful word was the word health.

I only stayed six days in the city of Ribeirão Preto, and I only ate one time at my aunt's house.

They didn't invite me to eat.

The young black girls dressed well. The men of color worked for the Antártica Company. My condition was pitiful. I had no home, nor work, and it's not at all pleasant to live out in the open. And everything in the world has its fate.

When a man is living, he has his house to shelter him, and when he dies, he has his tomb for his eternal rest. Remembering my chaotic past, the faces of the people I had known came into my mind. And I only missed my Grandfather, and my godmothers, Siá Maruca and Mariinha.

I remembered Dona Bárbara, Doutor Wanderley Andrade's mother-in-law. Her wrinkled face looked like a map. Can it be that the model for the map was the human face? It was friendly and sad, as if it were discontent with the world.

It's man who sows sadness in the world. My past returned to my mind as if it were a movie on the screen. What a horrible and hideous past! If I were to find a wallet full of money, who knows if my aunt wouldn't smile at me. Money isn't holy, but it also works miracles.

At the second house where I knocked and begged, the lady of the house said, "Go work, you bum!"

I became still. I, who have a fighting spirit of unwavering boldness, who am strong in my resolutions. I cried.

The word "bum" kept echoing in my brain as if it were the tick-tock of a clock. My tears were hot and they ran down my face, dripping on the ground. I thought, "I should die!" I kept walking until I found a park. I sat down and contemplated the clouds, thinking of my mother's house, so far away. There, I wasn't happy, my brother cursed me.

When the day was done, I went to my aunt's house.

They had already eaten dinner.

My aunt said to me, "They saw you seated in the park, and here in Ribeirão, decent people don't sit in the parks."

My cousin, José Marcelino, looked at me and said, "That is, decent people, but Bitita isn't decent." He was brushing his teeth and he asked me, "When is it that you're going to leave?" I didn't say anything. Say what? . . .

I got my bundle and left, cursing Aunt Ana.

I looked for the highway, intending to return to my home town on foot. I walked along, resigned. It was the beginning of my life, and fate was introducing me to the inhuman people who journey through this world. The kind who think they are immortal, devoid of beautiful qualities and have terrible moral foundations.

How many months would it take to arrive in Sacramento? I walked all day, thinking: when I find a lake or a river, I'm going to take a bath, five days without taking a bath! I have to be firm in my resolutions. I will never again speak with Aunt Ana's children. I will no longer consider them my relatives. If I am offended, I'm going to give back offense, like change.

What a struggle! I was hungry, but I was afraid to beg. At six o'clock I arrived in Jardinópolis. I looked for the Santa Casa, amazed.

All of the cities in the state of São Paulo have a Santa Casa, the *paulistas* are perfectionists. It seems like the only rich state in the country is the state of São Paulo.

I rang the bell thinking, "How will I be received?" And my heart began to beat faster as if I were dancing a *samba*. I felt like I had been given a shove and was being hurled out of the world. If I didn't recuperate my health, I would really have to beg. But it is so good to live by your own efforts! There is always someone who gives us work.

The door opened. A nun appeared. I thought, "They are very polite and understanding, you can get anything from them. They, who are outside of the world, know the world so well. And when they speak, we have the feeling they are prophetesses."

I asked, "Could you give me a treatment for my legs and arrange a place for me to take a bath, ma'am? I haven't taken a bath for five days. And this region is very hot. I stink."

The nun smiled and said, "You can come in. You are right, the human body must be washed every day and it must be fed. Our body is very costly to us. Where did you come from?"

"From Ribeirão. I am traveling to see if I can manage to heal these legs."

The sister smiled and said, "My daughter, in order to get well, rest is necessary. Not walking around from one place to another. You could even have been cured in your own home. You'd just go to the Santa Casa to be treated and bandaged up."

"In my home town, there isn't a Santa Casa."

I went to take a bath. What a relief, taking a bath in the bathroom with soap, hot water, and a towel to dry myself, a nightgown and a robe. What kindness. I was used to dealing with people as rough as cactuses.

And the sister, so soft! I thought, "Sisters are nice because they are educated, they're refined."

I went to dinner. I ate freely, without awkwardness. I felt tired, I went to bed.

I woke up at five o'clock with the warbling of the birds and the voices of the sisters praying the Hail Mary. While I slept, they had treated my legs. I got up and went to pray, to thank God for his benevolent intervention. I had breakfast and I went back to sleep. What a delight that clean bed was!

The sisters treated me as if I were a distinguished person. I told them that I had traveled to several cities, and I was now getting tired, "I'm convinced that I'm not going to achieve my goals."

The sister said that we can speak of the past, but that the future is unknown, it can surprise us with misfortune or with happiness.

In the infirmary, the women only spoke of the revolution. That it was beneficial to the people. That it had changed the lifestyle of the worker. There was a decent wage. They had the possibility of having a bank account. They named the advantages of the labor laws. The worker can retire in his old age and receive a full pension. The workers were happy with the laws. And Getúlio was already being dubbed "the father of the poor."

The people were disciplined. There were no conspiracies because the people weren't oppressed. They had the opportunity to get what they needed without being oppressed, without sacrificing themselves. Everyone dressed well. In the streets you couldn't tell who was poor, who was rich. Prices were within everyone's reach. What envy I felt because I couldn't work.

When I was little, I was healthy, and it's now that I was a young lady that I got sick. No one courted me, and men's scorn mortified me. It must be nice to kiss a man's face.

On visiting days, I stood watching, and was envious. Everyone had visitors except me.

"This is my mother."

"This is my aunt."

"This is my sister-in-law."

"This is my daughter and this is my husband."

Family ... something I don't have. When a sick woman was discharged, I cried. And the days went by.

My legs stayed the same. The sores didn't heal. I decided to leave the Santa Casa.

The sisters implored, "Stay! We have so much food and we have no one to eat it! We have no patients. Those who get sick here prefer to go to Ribeirão Preto, or São Paulo."

I thought, "If it were only possible for me to go to São Paulo for a consultation! ... But I have no resources. It's better that I go back to Sacramento, and it will be as God wills." I thanked the sisters, and I left.

When it got dark, I slept at the side of the road. Can it be that my life is going to be troubled like this? I don't want to beg. I don't want to steal. I want to be honest. I thought constantly and I didn't find a solution. The people who saw me walking along the roads kept looking and commenting, "She must be crazy!"

I stopped to rest and I heard a voice singing:

"When I drink
sometimes I find things strange,
sometimes I hit,
I also get beaten up.
When I drink,
I become rude,
I fight with my wife
and even with policemen.
When I drink
I become bad and a bully,
I fight with the army
and even with Lampeão.[2]
When I drink
I sleep around[3] *and even steal.*

---

2. Lampeão was the nickname given to Virgolino Ferreira da Silva (1898–1938), a famous bandit from the northeast of Brazil. He became a folk hero similar to Robin Hood, because he gained a reputation for stealing from the rich and giving to the poor.

3. The Portuguese expression "crio chifres," which we have translated here as "I sleep around," implies that he is having sexual relations with married women. The idea is that he is making cuckolds of their husbands.

I fight with the world
and even with the devil."

Looking at that man working the land I thought, "Would he give me work? I'm going to ask! Now I understood that the world is a collective. It's people needing each other." I asked him, "Mister! Do you need an employee? I can help you in the fields. You can pay me one thousand réis a day. It's that I'm sick and no one will give me work. I don't drink and I don't steal."

He stopped to listen to me and said that he could give me work. But his wife didn't work in the fields, "If you stay alone with me here, I'm afraid of wagging tongues."

I thought, "The tongue, such a small thing and so feared."

I'm no good at insisting. I decided to go on.

I was encouraging myself to fight, supported by my curiosity. I wanted to live to see what the better days that will come will bring me. When I read the lives of the saints, I noticed that the world wasn't cushy for them.

At four o'clock I arrived in the city of Sales de Oliveira. Walking through the streets I saw an announcement in the window of a house, "Servant wanted." I decided to ask for the job. I explained to the mistress that I could wash clothes, wax the floor, wash windows, and she could pay me twenty thousand réis a month. She hired me. What happiness! I would also have a mistress! I was no longer despised.

I cleaned the little room where I would sleep, feeling like I was in paradise. I hung up my dresses. I looked around the yard. It was large, but it didn't have one corner that was green or that had flowers.

At six o'clock, my employer arrived. He was a taxi driver. I ate dinner and went to sleep.

The next morning I noticed that it had rained. And if I had been on the road? That means that this was already one of my best days. I had breakfast and went to clean the yard. I washed the iron bars, the gate, and I polished the gate. I washed the clothes. I needed to please that mistress so that she wouldn't fire me. For me, that job was like a restorative tonic that was going to revive my morale. I felt like I was a nobody in this world. And I intended to be someone, and to be someone it's necessary to employ your time practicing some profession.

As the days went by, I came to know the names of my employers. She was Dona Maria Augusta. He was Arnaldo Padilha. She used to be a seamstress. She told me that she worked in São Paulo, in the Casa Alemã. She wanted to go back to São Paulo, she intended to put her girls in boarding school and work, she and her husband. But her husband didn't want to go to São Paulo, he loved life in the countryside.

She told me that she had gone to visit her godmother. And she made her get married. Marriage is an impediment[4] in a woman's life. She had no reason to be unhappy because Mr. Arnaldo Padilha was very well-bred.

I worked there for fifteen days. She told me that she had gotten a job for me in the city of Orlândia, "You have made the house very clean, now I can take care of everything by myself."

She gave me some necklaces and some earrings. It was the first necklace I ever wore in my life.

I was calm outside and crying inside. If only I could stay with her forever. What a beautiful woman. She looked like a doll. She spoke so little. And she knew how to speak. You could tell that she wasn't a lazy girl. Everything that she did turned out pretty. She gave me twenty thousand réis. What happiness! How long had it been since I had seen money! I got nervous. I didn't know where to keep it for fear of losing it.

At eleven o'clock the car that was going to take me to Orlândia arrived. I kept looking at the highway. What beauty!

When we arrived at the house where I was going to work, I saw two signs on the door: Dr. J. Manso Pereira. Dr. Mietta Santiago. I thought, "Can it be that they're going to hire me?" A mulatta appeared at the gate and invited me to come in. When I went into the garden, my heart began to beat fast as if it were warning me of something sinister. I tried to calm myself thinking, "Can it be that I'll be happy here?" Happiness is a myth created by man, it's nonexistent.

The house was on a corner. On the terrace, I saw several chairs and benches where the patients would sit. "What could it be that I'm going to do in this house? Wash, iron?"

The mulatta showed me a little room saying, "You're going to sleep there."

It was full of packing-boxes. I arranged the packing-boxes and

---

4. In the Portuguese, Carolina uses the word *redoma* here, which literally means a bell jar.

put the mattress in place. And I went to take a bath in order to go speak with the mistress.

She asked me my name, age, if I knew how to read and write, everything that I knew how to do, and she gave me paper, a pen, and the ink well. I wrote, "I know how to wash clothes, iron them, mend them, sew on buttons, make cakes, soap, sweets, stuff chickens, wax the floor." I gave her the note, she read it and praised my handwriting. I smiled because a doctor praised my calligraphy! When she saw me smile she said, "What snowy teeth!" I thought, "Can there be something wrong with my teeth?"

She told me that I should sweep the yard. I was ignorant and disorganized for work. There was plenty in the doctor's house. He examined me and treated my legs. I helped Raimunda take care of the house. How envious I was of her, who was strong and walked all over the city.

One day, rummaging through the packing-boxes, I found several books and a *Prosodic Dictionary* by João de Deus. It was the first time I had seen a dictionary. When I understood the purpose of a dictionary, I looked up the word "snowy," and I smiled, satisfied because I had an attractive feature: my teeth.

Raimunda told me about Belo Horizonte. It was Dr. Manso's mother who had raised her. Dona Segunda praised Dr. Manso's father.

Some days later, Dr. Manso's brother arrived. Another doctor who came to practice with his brother. Dr. Olinto Manso Pereira was tall. He was afraid of giving prescriptions!

He said, "God, help me get it right. My patient mustn't die. The death of a patient proves the incompetence of a doctor."

Raimunda cared for Dr. Mietta's son, Baby.[5] He wasn't baptized. His parents decided to wait until he grew up and he himself chose his name.

The employers decided to visit São Paulo. I asked Dr. Mietta to buy me some dresses. Raimunda wore a maid's uniform: a little cap and a white apron. Several people commented that that was ostentation. That that uniform was no longer used. That uniforms were from the time of the monarchy.

Raimunda was happy because she was going to get to know the renowned city of São Paulo. They stayed away for ten days.

---

5. In the original version, the English "Baby" is used.

When they returned, they spoke of the progress in the industrial city. But Dr. Mietta said that she intended to live in Rio de Janeiro. I didn't hear Dr. Manso's voice. He was a sad man. Why, if he was healthy, had a profession, a house, a wife, and a son? I was the one who should be sad. Dr. Mietta bought three dresses for me. What beautiful fade-proof fabrics. Dona Maria Augusta made the dresses. Ten cruzeiros each. I didn't pay it because I earned twenty thousand réis. I got tired of that life.

I decided to go on to Sacramento. I brought along the old books that were in the little room for me to read. When I arrived in my home-town, I was received hostilely by my relatives. I was now more intelligent and I observed the resentful faces. I thought, "They don't miss people."

My mother told me, "When you arrive, I already know that I'm going to have problems. Didn't I already tell you to stay there? It isn't meanness or dislike on my part, it's for your own good. It's a hard thing for me to watch them mistreat you."

But I, who in my wanderings slept under trees, was humiliated, I was now becoming desensitized. I showed her my dresses. She thought they were pretty. "This cloth is from São Paulo. It was my mistress who bought it."

"Oh, . . . you have a mistress? Don't be a liar. You say this, we're supposed to believe it, but we doubt it."

I showed her the necklaces. She chose a yellow one and left the green one for me.

I bought a parasol and noticed that my cousins envied my dresses. When they bought dresses, I didn't envy them.

18

Culture

What I didn't respect were useless vanities. They worked only to buy clothes. They could work to buy a piece of land and build a little house, which is the most important thing in life. I spent the days reading *The Lusiadas* by Camões,[1] with the help of the dictionary. I became more intellectual, understanding that an educated person knows how to tolerate life's afflictions.

Because I had taken lots of medicines, my legs were healing. I began making plans, "I'm going to get well. I'm going to get to know the city of São Paulo." The people said that it was the honeycomb city. In São Paulo, there's a neighborhood that's called Paradise. And the city of São Paulo is a paradise for the poor. It's the Brazilian state that has the most railroads.

Through books, I began becoming knowledgeable about the wars that there had been in Brazil, the War of the *Farrapos,*[2] the war with

---

1. A Portuguese epic poem honoring the deeds of the explorer Vasco da Gama (1460?-1524). It was written by Luis Vaz de Camões (1524?-1580) and published in 1572.

2. The War of the *Farrapos* means roughly the "War of the Ragamuffins." It was a revolt that broke out in Rio Grande do Sul in 1835 against the central government of Brazil. It was partially incited by the belief on the part of the *gaúchos* that, despite their significant economic contributions to the nation, they were burdened by heavy taxes. The name *farrapos* is apparently a reference to the clothing that the Brazilian revolutionary Cipriano Barata chose to wear in Lisbon prior to independence, which he topped off with a straw hat in order to distinguish himself from the Portuguese as a Brazilian. The adversaries of the *farrapos* gave them this name as an insult.

Paraguay. I condemned this brutal and inhuman method that man had found to resolve his problems.

I sat in the sun to read. The people passing by looked at the dictionary and said, "What a thick book! It must be the book of Saint Cyprian."[3]

It was the only book that the ignorant people knew existed and exists. They began to spread the word that I had a book of Saint Cyprian. And they commented, "So, she's studying to be a witch in order to mess up our lives. A sorcerer prays, and it doesn't rain; a sorcerer prays, and the frost comes."

When my mother found out, she warned me, "It's better that you stop reading these books, they are already saying that it's the book of Saint Cyprian, that you're a sorceress."

I gave a stentorian laugh. People who become enlightened and prudent know how to conduct themselves in life, "I want to get well in order to leave here and never come back."

I was happy because the sores were healing. I wanted to surprise my mother. I was following the advice of the sister from Jardinópolis. If I rested in my own home, I could heal myself. In my house I was peaceful. I didn't become enraged, I didn't feel that inner anguish. When I wasn't reading, I embroidered something.

My brother, who wandered around from here to there, appeared. What pity I felt for those poor young men. They couldn't stay in the city because the police persecuted them. The poor men looked at the police like cats looked at dogs. But this is ignorance, because the man who's a policeman is also poor, and he knows the difficulties that a poor man faces to live. The beehive of the poor produces bitter honey.

One day I was reading, some young men passed by, they stopped and asked to see my dictionary. I gave them the book for them to look at. They looked at it and said, "Oh! So it's really the book of Saint Cyprian. How heavy it is."

I realized that they were pretentious and I felt sorry for them because reading benefits men as much as women. I complained that my wish was to be healthy in order to work. That illness had transformed me into human rubbish.

3. The book of St. Cyprian is a book of magic. It includes prayers, spells, and hexes designed to enable its user to do such things as cure illness, re-attract errant lovers, and wreak vengeance on enemies.

When they left, they went to tell the sergeant that I had called him rubbish, saying that they only arrested the poor. The sergeant was my cousin Leonor's *compadre,* and he gave the military policemen the order to go arrest me. I was at home. I didn't like to go out because I was irritated by the gossip surrounding my name.

I was aware of the fact that the rich who are born in small cities can be born naked, but the poor have to be born dressed in patience in order to put up with ignorance. I was scared when I saw the policemen. They stopped in front of me and said I was under arrest. I didn't ask why I was being arrested. I merely obeyed. My mother interfered, saying that I wasn't doing anything wrong, "Shut up! And you're also under arrest."

We went along in front of the two policemen.

My mother cried saying, "I told you not to come to this city. Why don't you stay with the *paulistas*?"

When we arrived at the jail, the people already knew that I was being arrested. They put us into a cell. I thought of the nun who advised me, "Go to your hometown, and there you will rest and get well. You don't have the temperament to be confined."

We were imprisoned for two days without eating. On the third day, the sergeant made us weed in front of the jail. People passed by on the street without seeing us.

I thought, "I accept the fact that a fair punishment be given to those who make mistakes, but I didn't make a mistake." On the fourth day, we weeded until noon. My hands hurt, the sores flared up again due to the lack of medicine.

At one o'clock in the afternoon, they came to get us and the sergeant began to interrogate me, "So, you're going around saying that I'm rubbish?"

I understood, "Oh, so it was Li who told."

"I told Li that illness was transforming me into human rubbish. And I consider myself inferior to others. I don't like it when they say to me, 'You festering woman!' It's not my fault that I'm sick. When I get well, I want to work."

"You've been reading the book of Saint Cyprian. Who do you intend to put a spell on?"

"I don't believe in spells and I don't have the book of Saint Cyprian."

"I have it."

And he gave me the book to look at and page through. I liked books immensely and handled the book with tenderness and care, as if I were handling a new-born child. But I was nervous to read it.

"They say that you go out at night and go wandering around the city."

My mother said, "She doesn't go out at night."

"Shut up, tramp!"

We returned to the cell.

The sergeant ordered a black military policeman to beat us. He beat us with a rubber club. My mother wanted to protect me, she put her arm in front of me, taking the blows. Her arm broke, she fainted, I went to help her, the soldier continued to beat me. Five days imprisoned and without eating.

My aunt came to visit us and she brought a dish of shredded meat with manioc flour. My legs swelled up. I thought, "These guys must be the descendants of Nero, who was a fanatic for cruelty." My mother's arm hurt. She cried. A soldier named Isaltino cursed me, "This tramp is always traveling. A decent young woman doesn't travel. She says she's going to São Paulo."

I asked my aunt to go speak with Mr. Aureslino de Campos, the manager of the bank, to have me released. I would pay him afterward. He told me that he couldn't, I had to pay prison costs, twenty thousand réis.

My legs began to stink. I thought, "And if they get worms?"

My cousin Paulo got together the twenty thousand réis and had me released. I will consider my cousin Paulo as my only relative.

The sores became inflamed. My mother couldn't do laundry. We went walking around the countryside begging. My mother with her broken arm and I with my bandaged legs. We got rice, beans, salt pork, soap, cheese, leftover food.

My mother said, "You need to leave this city."

"All right," I agreed.

I thought of the generosity of the *paulistas*.

Family men prohibited their daughters from talking to me. I would contaminate them with bad examples.

We left the city of Sacramento. We went to Franca. What a struggle for me to live in Franca. I couldn't work. My mother got a job in Mr. Ignácio Calheiros's house. I was left wandering. What hunger I suffered!

Sometimes, I went to my mother's workplace. I cleaned the yard, seeking to eat something! We didn't have a house. We would sleep at Chicolim's little ranch. He was a broken-down circus clown and well on in years. He was charitable. He was the father of the actress Carmem Cassnel. What a good man!

19

The Safe

I was an outraged woman. I began to travel, seeking treatment. I got well. What happiness! My mother smiled.

I got a job. I went to work at the "Three Brothers" farm for Dona Clélia. She would pay me forty thousand réis a month. What a refined woman, she could be an actress or a movie star.

Everything that I did for her, I did with great care and tenderness. It wasn't to butter her up. It was out of kindness and consideration.

What plenty! For me, a grain of rice had the value of a diamond. I needed to revive my soul that was incredulous of everything.

When I got the twenty-five thousand réis, I smiled and cried because Dona Clélia's former servant returned, saying that she only liked to work for her. Dona Clélia was the daughter of Italians, married to Mr. Abdo, a Syrian. He knew how to speak Arabic.

With health, there is no lack of work, and I became less inhibited. I could wear socks. No one was nauseated by me. I got a job in Mr. Emílio Bruxelas's house. He was married to Dona Zizinha. What a serious woman! She made an effort to get along well with her stepsons, Sinésio, Ibraim, and the others. When she cooked, I watched in order to learn because I intended to be a big shot in the kitchen.

Mr. Bruxelas bought a safe in São Paulo. When the safe arrived, I was sweeping the living room. The man who delivered the safe explained the secret! "You turn it three times, zero. Turn it four times, two."

I wasn't paying much attention to the explanation, but the information got recorded in my mind.

Mr. Emílio Bruxelas took the paper, read it, and closed the safe. And he turned the numbers again, the safe opened. He took his valuable objects, papers, documents, and a pile of money and put them in the safe saying, "Now I am really calm, I can leave home in peace. This safe, thieves won't manage to open."

Dona Zizinha, who was expecting her first child, walked into the living room and asked me to make the coffee. After having coffee, the man who delivered the safe said good-bye. Some days later, Mr. Emílio Bruxelas lost the paper that had the explanation for opening the safe. He became upset. Mr. Jozias de Almeida told him, "Carolina is very intelligent. If she heard the secret of the safe, she must have memorized it."

Then, Mr. Emílio Bruxelas decided to find out, and he looked for me in the kitchen and he stared at me. That look made me uncomfortable, I felt like I was in front of an X-ray. I understood that he wanted to tell me something.

It was raining. I was cold, but I didn't have warm clothing, or any hope of having any.

He asked me, "Did you see the safe?"

"Yes, sir, I saw it!"

"Mr. Jozias de Almeida told me that you're very intelligent."

How happy I felt. Wow, whites remarking that I'm intelligent! This, for me, is an honor. So, they spoke about me out there.

But there must be a reason, because those men would only talk about the price of coffee, commenting about the time when Getúlio ordered that the surplus be burned, which hurt the Nation. Even if they sold the coffee for a lower price, there was still a profit. Burning it was a total loss. Many families became poor. Mr. Emílio continued, "Did you hear the man read the secret of the safe?"

"Yes, sir, I heard."

"Would you be able to write down what it was that you heard?"

I became proud, "Oh! Yes, I can!"

He took a piece of paper and gave it to me.

I wrote, "Turn it three times, zero. Turn it four times, two."

I wrote down what I had heard and I gave it to him. He went

running to open the safe. It opened. He went looking for me in the kitchen, "Dona Carolina, you can go away now. Get your clothes together and leave."

I was frightened because it was raining. I couldn't ask him why it is that he was kicking me out of his house if I had done him a great favor, helping him open the safe. My pride spoke louder. Since he's kicking me out, I'm going to leave without asking for an explanation. He gave me thirty thousand réis and I left. I had no umbrella. I took five steps, I got soaked. There was no one on the streets. I had no home. What a struggle!

When I got to Dolores's house I was soaking wet. I didn't want to bother her. I was already unhappy about being classified as inferior. What a relief when day broke.

I went to wring out my clothes, wondering where to get another job. There were many people who needed to work. I didn't demand a high price. Because of the rain, I began to cough.

I went to work at Mr. Teófilo's house, they sent me away because of the cough. I thought that if I regained my health, I would live like an aristocrat. I was mistaken. The days for me were still unhappy and tragic. My dreams didn't come true. I wanted to work in order to take care of my mother.

The good jobs were already filled by people who looked better. I decided to look for work outside of the city. On the farms. In the farmers' houses.

20

The Medium

I went to work for Dona Maria Amélia, Totonho Rasa's daughter, Mr.
Roberto Junqueira's wife. What a well-bred mistress! I was Nilza's
nurse. What a pretty little girl. She was sick. Dona Maria Amélia was
sad. I wondered, "Why, if she's rich?"

We returned to the city. Dr. Carlos Signareli began to treat the little
girl. How I liked Dona Maria Amélia! I thought, "If she doesn't fire
me, I'll stay with her always." She spoke very elegantly. Looking at
her, she seemed like a princess.

The little girl was dying, and she, as well. Dr. Carlos Signareli said
that it was meningitis. Dona Maria Amélia's mother fired me, saying
that she didn't like me.

When I left that house, I prayed, asking God to help Dona Maria
Amélia who had all of the qualities necessary to be canonized.

I found another job in a boarding house. But I wasn't able to forget
Dona Maria Amélia Junqueira. I prayed, asking God that the little girl
not die and that she not suffer. And I went to Our Lady of Conception
church, I stopped before the altar, begging the saints that they not
allow Nilza to die. How I missed the little girl!

I swore never again to be a nurse because, through intimacy, we
learn to love the children. But Nilza died.

I didn't have any clothes to wear. I wrote a note to Dona Maria

Amélia, asking her for her used dresses. She gave me them. I wrote the note with confidence that she wouldn't say no.

When I like a person, I like to see her every day. I wanted to see Dona Maria Amélia because I missed her, and I didn't want to see her because she must be very sad because of Nilza's death.

What a hit when I put on the dresses that Dona Maria Amélia gave me! Yellow organdy. Full of frills. I thought, "If I could always dress like this!" And I went dancing.

It was horrible to live. I was working, earning thirty thousand réis, another woman appeared who worked better and earned twenty thousand réis a month. I was already tired of that wandering life. I felt like I was a circulating coin. How ashamed I felt because we didn't have a house.

We rented a room in Dona Narcisa's house. The price of the room was fifty thousand réis a month. What a struggle to get together these fifty thousand réis in order to pay the first month in advance. We had no peace, wondering, "Is it possible that we're going to get together enough money to pay the second month? If no one had a steady job." My mother looked at me and said, "I can't trust you. I've already realized that you're never going to be able to help me."

We slept on the ground. We covered the ground with newspapers.

My mother said, "We've become gypsies. It's horrible to be here today, there tomorrow. We are just like circus people."

I felt as if I were a piece of trash. A weak currency, without value. We couldn't buy anything to eat. When the month was up, we couldn't pay. We walked away before the black woman kicked us out.

Dolores got a boyfriend and went to live with him. She took my mother. I cried and left on foot, with my little bundle in my arms. Arriving with no money was disgraceful. But I only know how to get money honestly. When I arrived in the city, I waited for night to fall to enter the city.

Later, I went to look for Dolores, who was sick. A pain in her eyes. My mother was very thin, complaining of pain in her stomach. I saw several people go to São Paulo and I thought, "My turn will come." I had already been working for a year and I hadn't even earned a hundred thousand réis. I envied those young women who earned sixty thousand réis a month.

To my unhappiness, I got sick. What a fever I had. I had dysentery. I groaned day and night.

Lying in the hall of Chicolim's little farm, one night I heard a car stop and someone ask, "Is it here that there's a sick woman?"

They said yes. And Mr. Arnulfo de Lima came in, looked at me, and said to me, "So, it's really you."

He said that he was sleeping in his house and my spirit went to ask him for help: a mattress and a doctor to examine me. I still hadn't finished my life cycle and it wasn't time for me to leave my body. I gave him my address.

I knew Mr. Arnulfo de Lima. He was the owner of a Spiritualist center. He brought a doctor to examine me. He gave me an injection. I was lying on the floorboards. What delight to lie down on that mattress! I went to sleep.

I woke up at nine in the morning with my body hot, feeling like I was being roasted alive. I got scared. I filled a tub with cold water, I got in. What relief! What a pleasant feeling! When I got out of the water, it was hot. And the sickness disappeared.

Until today I don't understand this mystery of going to look for the medium Arnulfo de Lima. He didn't know me. But I prayed for him to be happy. I felt like I wasn't awake, like I was dreaming. I wanted to look for Mr. Arnulfo de Lima, but I had no clothes. I wondered, "Why is it that my spirit didn't seek out Dr. Tomaz Nortelino, who's a Spiritualist?" I began to understand that I receive protection, and I don't know its origin. But I was happy. How good a sound body is! I went to look for work, I felt like I had taken a restorative tonic.

It was the year 1936. The people said that they were getting rich with Getúlio's way of governing the country. The taxes weren't onerous. In all of the bars and other establishments was hung the portrait of our distinguished head of state. The merchants, when they did the books, had a favorable balance. The prices were stable from year to year. When the worker received his money, it was already designated for this or for that. What a happy people!

21

The Mistress

I was happy when I got a job on a farm. I couldn't work in the city because I had no clothes. In the countryside, anything will do. Life is simple, without bureaucracy. I went to work on Mr. Nhonhô Rasa's farm. He was deaf. But very polite to the farmhands. I was a nurse-maid. How much milk, cheese, and vegetables! The servants criticized me saying, "You're an idiot, leaving the city to come work in the sticks."

When the mistress would go to the city, I would go along to take care of the children. She would go out, going to the movies to have a little fun.

I wanted a more active job. And sitting around with a child in my arms all day was tiring me. I felt like time wasn't passing. I wondered, "How can my mother be living?" I got tired of that stagnant life. A life without a promising tomorrow. I felt tremendous discontent. What longing to have a house, a settled life!

The mistress was great. I was ashamed to say that I wanted to quit the job. My wish was to live in the city, to go to the movies. To dance, to join a group of *carnaval* revelers, "Just to get worn out." It was Benedito Musa's group. But when I went to ask him if he would accept me in his group, he told me, "I wouldn't even accept you to polish my girls' shoes. No beggars can join my group. You have no clothes."

He was right, but I became upset.

My dream was to dance to the music of the jazz band Bico Doce, from Ribeirão Preto. For me, my life was like a rock that I couldn't lift. From thinking so much I began acquiring the habit of not complaining, not lamenting. Why torture myself with the impossible?

The boss was friendly, he teased the workers. I though it was funny when he said, "Good morning, corkscrew!"

What order on that farm! The workers wanted to leave the farm, but they didn't have the nerve to ask for their wages. The politeness of the bosses and the children stopped us.

The workers were treated as if they were family. Mr. Nhonhô played *caipira*[1] records for the farmhands and said, "It's outdated to treat employees with disdain."

When I told Dona Fiica that I wanted to leave, she didn't appreciate it and asked me, "What is it that you're lacking here? Tell me what you want and I'll take care of it."

I thought, "I'm going to ask her to buy me some clothes. But if she buys them, I'll have to stay with her. I'm already getting tired of living in the country. If it were meant for me to live on this farm to plant, then yes. But I hope that God will yet help me, I will have lands to plant. I will have the life that I hope to have."

Dona Fiica said to me, "You know, Carolina, many people fought for the freedom of you people. But you people aren't attached to anything. You seem like squirrels. I find you, the blacks, a very difficult people. If you are disorganized, it's because you want to be. What is it that you gain by your wanderings? It seems like you come into our houses only to investigate something, and then you leave. I can live in the city, but the city doesn't entice me. I'm already familiar with everything. Here I can raise my children more comfortably and with less expense. Living in the city, I have to buy supplies by the kilo, and I don't like it."

In the kitchen there were two cooks. What plenty!

She said to me, "When I go to the city, I'll take you and drop you off there, you are already used to sleeping in buildings condemned by city hall."

Our conversation ended when we heard Mr. Nhonhô's voice. I went to serve lunch.

---

1. *Caipira* refers here to Brazilian country music. The term *caipira* itself is roughly equivalent to "hick" in English.

The cook wanted to leave and it had already been a year that she'd been saying, "Tomorrow, I'll say that I want to leave. Tomorrow, I'll say that I want to leave."

I felt like Dona Fiica had taken a course in being a mistress. When she went to the city, she took me by automobile. She said to me, "I could let you come on foot. But I feel sorry for you. I don't like to hurt anyone."

She paid me, I divided the money with my mother. I was ashamed to give her only twenty thousand réis. I looked at the money and I thought, "Without this paper, no one lives. It controls us and it predominates in our lives. Those who have a lot are strong, are respected, are the masters of the ship; whoever doesn't have it in great quantities is a Joe Nobody, an underdog, they are the disregarded, they are the weak." I only managed to eat when I was employed. It was necessary to look for a job in order to live always in the city.

22

Being a Cook

I was lucky and I went to work in a wealthy house. What a sumptuous, palatial house! What longing to live in a pretty house and be the lady of that house. It was an impossible dream. I felt like I was superfluous in this world.

My mother asked me to get together some money because she was going to return to Sacramento, "But don't you ever return to that city again."

My objective was to get together the fifty thousand réis. And in that house I was going to earn sixty a month. I would be a cook. I cooked. The first day, the boss complained. He asked for more care. The food wasn't tasty.

I was mortified. I, who intended to be a good cook.

I was sluggish. I didn't manage to wash all of the dishes and take care of the food. The mistress would say to me, "It seems like you're not used to working. Hurry up, because you have to slaughter a chicken."

I didn't know how to slaughter fowl. But even so, I slaughtered it. I didn't manage to cut up the pieces. The mistress complained. After a great struggle, dinner was ready.

I wanted to quit the job. I understood that I wasn't up to the work. And I didn't know how to cook well enough. I began to hear irate voices, "Wretch." "Bitch, disgusting woman!" I got scared when I looked at the mistress's face, "Pack your clothes and leave!"

How I feared that mistress! In the beginning I already understood that she wasn't satisfied with my work. I was leaving with my bundles. I met the mistress's son, who had just arrived. Hearing his mother curse me, he said to her, "Oh, Mama! One doesn't treat the servants like that. They're also human beings who deserve our respect."

The mother explained to him, "It's that this little nigger woman slaughtered a chicken and didn't take out the gizzard."

The mistress's son laughed.

I thought, "Oh! That's why she fired me." The gossip circulated through the city: a cook who didn't take the gizzards out of the fowl. What protected me is that the mistress didn't memorize my name. And I didn't get to know the inhabitants of that house properly.

When I was on the street I became uncertain. I didn't know where to go. I was afraid to seek out relatives. They looked at me as if I were responsible for their misfortunes. I went looking for Maria Vacabrava's[1] house. She would take me in because sometimes I shared my money with her. In certain circumstances, money replaces judgment. She was so nasty, pretentious, she was illiterate and she wanted to speak classically. She was constantly memorizing difficult words. She was attractive because of her snowy teeth. When we spoke, she criticized me, "You have no aspirations, you were born already old. You have nowhere to live. You go around badly dressed. If I could, I would like to live in Rio de Janeiro. What a pleasant city!"

She got together some rags, and I lay down, lamenting my life. I couldn't tolerate that smell of *cachaça* and cigarettes.

I woke up and left, promising myself that I would be a good cook. I would make an effort to be sought after and not thrown out.

In the Santa Casa, they were looking for a cook. What luck! I rejoiced. I applied.

The sister hired me, she asked for references, but my mistresses were farmers' wives. It was hard to locate them.

The sister decided to hire me and she told me, "You will prove your abilities."

I thought, "Can it be that I have some useful abilities?"

I was to sleep in the Santa Casa. What a very clean bed! Nightgowns for me to change into. Electric lights. The sister who helped me

---

1. *Vaca-brava* literally means "wild cow."

in the kitchen was Sister Irinéia, who asked me, "How often have you gone to dances?"

I thought! I thought and responded, "About thirty times, I think."

"Oh! So that means you like to dance!"

"Well, like it, not really. But my girlfriends would invite me persistently. In order not to upset them, then I go. You know that people host dances in their homes. When a lot of people show up, then the dance is lively."

I waited for her to ask me another question. As she didn't say anything, I kept doing my work. We served lunch. First in the poor people's infirmary. Then to the patients in the ward. When the plates returned, I found out that the food was appreciated. I washed the dishes quickly. I kept the kitchen very clean. I didn't want to be chastised or fired.

I was happy when I got a visit from the mother superior. She came to tell me that the food was well-prepared. That it was necessary to vary it more. In the kitchen there was a cookbook, I read it at night. I thought about my life that was improving. What a salary! Eighty thousand réis a month. It was the best salary in the city. I congratulated myself, analyzing my rise in status. I understood that I would depend on myself to struggle to succeed.

I learned how to make several dishes with Sister Irinéia. What plenty! What a lot of milk! With that comforting food, I began to put on weight. I was very careful with my personal cleanliness because Sister Irinéia complained about everything. And I, fearing the sister's comments, sought to perfect myself. I had the prestige that I had desired for a long time. The prestige of a good servant.

I felt like a general who had won a hard-fought battle and was now being decorated. I was no longer afraid of the world, and not of life, either. I understood that a careless, disorganized, lazy person doesn't manage to win in life. It depended on my adopting good qualities. And I kept analyzing the facts. Bad people have to separate themselves from evil in order to fit in in this world. The dishonest, to follow honesty. Because the dishonest are those who have no conscience, they only look out for their own well-being. The strong should guide and enlighten the unwise, the ignorant. I had no one to guide me in this life. What prevented me from falling into the abyss were Grandpa's words, "You should not steal! The man who steals no longer has any chance of rehabilitating himself. We shouldn't deceive those who put their trust in us. When you enter a house, make a good impression so that you will be able to return again and be greeted with smiles. Those who take other people's things are buying their tickets to visit hell."

I don't have kleptomaniac tendencies, so I am yet going to be happy. I didn't come into the world through the living room. I came in through the back door. I would succeed because I was different.

I would get out of bed at 5 o'clock, would prepare the patients' morning meal. The work was easy, I didn't get tired. And the salary motivated me. It was as if I had left a garret to live in a mansion.

In the morning, the nuns would go into the kitchen, they greeted me, "Christ's blessing, sister."

"May He be forever praised."

The nicest was Sister Maria José. What personality! She had all of the qualities that a sensible woman should have. Looking at her I thought, "She could have made someone a good wife. She could be a teacher, a journalist, and an actress." My dream was to put her on an altar and adore her as if she were a saint.

I took care of the kitchen as if it were a golden alcove. When Sister Irinéia would come in, I would notice that she didn't like me. But her coldness didn't affect me. I was already learning to look at the practical side of life. And that salary controlled me as if it were a bit. She would praise my predecessor, would say that she was very funny. My predecessor was Vitório's wife. The most polite black man in the city of Franca, but he was in prison because they discovered he was a thief.

Sister Irinéia asked me, "Have you ever been to church?"

"A few times."

I responded, a little confused because I already knew that after the questions came a comment. I felt like I was in combat, and that I should keep my guard up. Prepared to receive a blow.

"So, you've been to dances many times and to church a few times?"

I was quiet.

I wasn't enticed by that conversation. I prepared lunch.

I was very happy because, on my day off, my friends looked at me enviously. My salary was commented on all throughout the city.

My mother smiled saying, "God decided to help you. I believe that He heard my prayers. Mothers don't like to see their children suffering."

When I got paid, I gave my mother fifty thousand réis, she returned to Sacramento. And I kept thirty thousand réis. I felt like I was rich.

I took account of my aspirations: I intended to buy a palatial house, to buy very fine clothes, unattainable desires. I should get those dreams of grandeur out of my head. I wanted to buy clothes to compete with my cousins. I was depressed because of having suffered a lot. But now I should adopt my own lifestyle, "I am going to live within my means without ostentation. Understanding that any work that we do will be easier with dedication." I intended to restrain my vanity.

During my break, I asked the sister for permission to go out, I went to buy a dress. What inner happiness! I intended to have several dresses.

Dona Agostinha made the dress. Cut on the bias. How good it is to see our desires fulfilled! That dress had the effect of a magical spell on my subconscious. It was like a restorative tonic for my feminine pride.

I asked myself, "Can it be that I'll look pretty when I wear it?" In order to wear it, I should go to a party. Or wear it to go out with a boyfriend. I was doubly happy. Now I could go to dances without awkwardness.

I grabbed the broom and went dancing in the kitchen, which was spacious. I felt like I was wearing my dress. When I whirled around, I met Sister Irinéia's eyes, staring at me. They were large, oval eyes. Black and shiny, as if they were varnished. I stopped suddenly, put the broom back, and went to see to the pans.

The sister said to me, "I think you should be a dancer, and not a cook."

I forgot about the dress, the parties, and dedicated myself to my work.

The sisters were getting ready to travel to São Paulo, they were going to go on a retreat. There were six sisters, they traveled in pairs.

To be honest, I began to miss having fun, so I decided to leave. I might make less in another house, but I could go out on Sundays, go to the movies, and have fun. I asked for my wages. After I had left the job, I understood my foolishness . . .

Dolores, my cousin, cursed me, "You're an ass. Idiot. You were earning almost one hundred thousand réis a month and you had the nerve to leave. We have to learn to look at the advantages."

I had some money, and I went to fulfill my dream. I went to the movies, wearing my new dress. I went to visit Dona Clélia, and she got me a job in her sister-in-law Dona Salima's house. Washing and ironing. Taking care of the house when she was in the store. Some days later, her son José traveled to São Paulo in order to study in the Syrian-Brazilian School, on Paulista Avenue.

I thought, "The poor go to São Paulo to live, the young people go to São Paulo to be educated in order to transform themselves into tomorrow's good Brazilians."

I didn't tell my relatives where I was working. And I didn't go out because there was too much work. I was left alone to take care of everything.

One Sunday I went to visit Dolores, she was sick again, a milk-colored liquid was streaming out of her eyes. The illness was controlling her. I pitied her.

She told me that she had received letters from my mother. That the police were beating up on my Uncle Antônio. I kept thinking about my family, they were all illiterate and they couldn't live in the big cities. And the only thing that I could do for them was merely pity them.

I answered my mother's letter, asking her not to talk. The poor have to be voiceless. To live in our own country as if we were foreigners. The fury of the law against us was bitter. The law can be severe. But with some help, it can be beneficial. A child is arrested, but made to study. A young man is arrested, but taught a trade, readapting him to society. If a man is the father of numerous offspring, the country can help him educate his children—this was one of the dreams of the late lamented Rui Barbosa who said that the people need a leader or a king. That a mediocre king makes the people work to fill his coffers. But a wise king works for the well-being of his people. That anyone can govern an upright and noble people. That an excess of freedom eclipses authority in the home, the schools, and the workplace. That someone is always the authority over someone else. That a man is a leader in his home with his wife and children, the boss with his employees. This is a rule of humanity.

I worked for Dona Salima for three months, I was going to earn forty thousand réis a month. When the month was up, I was embarrassed to charge her. When ninety days were up, I decided to charge her. She only gave me ten thousand réis. I said, "That's it?" She responded, "If you aren't happy, you can leave my house."

I cried thinking about the quantity of clothing I had washed and ironed. Taking care of the yard, looking after the house when she was absent. I didn't steal. I took care of everything as if it were mine. I decided to look for another job. Or leave the countryside.

I intended to find a job with better remuneration. I had to learn to react, to demand that people honor my labor contracts. But, I had no home and I was already tired of my wandering life.

The mistress was a foreigner, and I, a national. I couldn't compete with her. She was rich, and I, poor. She could have me arrested. I continued working.

The mistress smiled, saying that she had found an idiot who worked almost for free. After dinner, I went out walking around the city, looking for a job. I was healthy. There was no obstacle to hinder me.

They told me about a teacher who was looking for a maid to come to São Paulo. I went looking for her, she hired me. What happiness! I went running back, began packing my clothes. I didn't tell the mistress that I was going to leave, she had already fired me.

Finally, I was going to get to know the celebrated city of São Paulo! I sang as I worked because all of the people who are going to live in the capital of the state of São Paulo rejoice as if they were going to heaven.

On the day of the trip, I didn't go to sleep so that I wouldn't miss the train. The train was leaving at seven o'clock, but I arrived at the station at five o'clock. What happiness when I boarded!

When I arrived in the capital, I liked the city because São Paulo is the axis of Brazil. It's the spinal column of our country. How many politicians! What a progressive city. São Paulo should be the model so that this country might transform itself into a good Brazil for Brazilians.

I prayed, thanking God and asking Him for protection. Who knows, I might find a way to buy a little house and live the rest of my days in peace . . .

Afterword

Just as had occurred with *Casa de Alvenaria* and her subsequent books following the unprecedented success of her first diary, *Quarto de Despejo,* Carolina Maria de Jesus's autobiographical *Diário de Bitita* sold poorly when it appeared in 1986. Critics dismissed it as irrelevant. Several reasons explain this. The mid-1980s were a time of tension in Brazil over the return to civilian rule after two decades of military dictatorship, and for complex reasons, Brazilian readers did not consider Carolina's story of her childhood squalor worthy of comment or debate. In the years since Carolina's death in 1977, moreover, many Brazilians had come to believe the untruthful supposition spread about Carolina in 1960 when *Quarto* had been published: that she could not have written something as perceptive as her diaries and that therefore they must have been the work of Dantas, her Svengali. This interpretation continued to be held even into the early 1990s, when new evidence was brought to light attesting to the authenticity of her written work and the fact that she had written thousands of diary entries and other writings neither published nor known to persons beyond her family.[1]

Asked to comment on the importance of Carolina Maria de Jesus's

---

1. See José Carlos Sebe Bom Meihy and Robert M. Levine, *Meu Estranho Diário* (São Paulo: Editorial Xamã, 1996).

writing, many Brazilians continued to equivocate. One wrote of feeling "uncomfortable" with the "risk of exoticism—a poor black woman in an underdeveloped country writing diaries in a naif style and becoming a best-selling author."[2] Perhaps the most telling reason for the failure of Brazilians to consider Carolina Maria de Jesus's life as important was the traditional notion that men and women are born to their class and, with the sole exception of a tiny handful of soccer stars and musicians, know their place and stay in it. It is ironic that while Brazil boasts the most relaxed racial environment of any country in the world, the elite shows little interest in stories of life's travails. In the United States, dramatic rags-to-riches stories capture headlines, even if they do not happen very often. In 1997, Jessie Lee Brown Foveaux, a black Kansas woman who reared eight children while working in a laundry and as a nurse's aide and who wrote the story of her life, received at the age of ninety-eight more than a million dollars for the rights to her memoir. The *Life of Jessie Lee Brown from Birth Up to 80* was called a "literary sensation" by the *New York Times* for her account of her lifelong struggles to cope with hardship. "I made up my mind to live my life so that I need not be ashamed to look at myself in the mirror," she said. Her editor at Warner Books, her publisher, considered her manuscript the "very plain, very clear" writing of an everyday heroine. "We're not going to touch [edit] it because we feel it's evocative and emotionally powerful," the editor said.[3]

In contrast, Brazilian intellectuals continued to recognize no value in Carolina's writing, which they insisted on judging as literature rather than as the expression of a voice from the otherwise silent underclass. Since Carolina wrote in an old-fashioned hand marked by odd spellings, occasional misuse of language, and frequent repetition, and because she also held stubbornly to a personal outlook which people considered selfish, it was convenient for critics to deny her significance, sometimes in ways that were cruel. Not only did traditionalists like Wilson Martins scoff at her diaries as "literary hoaxes," but they mocked foreign academics for using Carolina's writings in

2. Anonymous written statement by a self-described "Brazilian intellectual," to Robert M. Levine, May 7, 1997.

3. Claire Zion, quoted in the *New York Times,* March 24, 1997, A1, C7. It is interesting that Penguin USA, the publisher of Carolina Maria de Jesus's first diary's English translation, *Child of the Dark,* turned down the manuscript although its editor called the writing "pretty rough, but absolutely compelling."

their classrooms.[4] When two new volumes about Carolina appeared in 1995—*Antologia Pessoal,* a collection of her unpublished poems, and *Meu Estranho Diário,* an analysis of Carolina's unedited diary entries—Marilene Felinto, the cultural page reviewer for the prestigious daily newspaper *Folha de São Paulo,* attacked Carolina's writing as "clichés born in the *favela,*" and criticized the new works as a failed attempt at "giving literary stature to Carolina de Jesus."[5] Although these books sold fairly well, the intellectual establishment seemed unwilling to accept Carolina for what she was and not to judge her for what she was not: a politically correct revolutionary seeking solidarity with left-wing political movements and leading her fellow *favelados* to the barricades.

Not only did Felinto reject Carolina's writing exclusively because she considered it bad, immature literature, but her dismissal of any other arguments for considering Carolina a significant voice from the depths of Brazilian society was all the more disheartening to non-Brazilians because Felinto is black herself, one of a tiny handful of blacks who have achieved intellectual stature.[6] Wilson Martins's hostility is ironic because much of his career as a teacher and literary critic was spent in the United States, at cosmopolitan New York University. The reason that Martins had to leave Brazil is instructive as well. In December 1968, just as Brazil's military dictatorship had started to tighten its repression, Martins became involved in a personal feud with Audálio Dantas. Shortly afterward, Martins left for the United States. The memory of the quarrel may have motivated Martins more than two decades later to attack *Quarto de Despejo* (and therefore attack Dantas's reputation as much as Carolina's) when it was republished in a new, low-budget edition in 1993 aimed at school pupils. The republication of the 1960 diary had little impact: four years later, the large majority of Brazilian university students had never heard of Carolina de Jesus.

---

4. Wilson Martins, in *Jornal do Brasil* and other newspapers, October 23, 1995, and "Lendo Carolina," in newspapers across Brazil, April 29, 1995.

5. Marilene Felinto, "Clichés Nascidos na Favela," *Folha de São Paulo,* September 29, 1996, 11, in the newspaper's literary supplement, *Caderno Mais!.*

6. On the paucity of blacks in intellectual and university life in Brazil, see Paulo Sérgio Pinheiro's interview with Carolina Domingo and Michael J. Francis in the *Newsletter of the Kellogg Institute* (University of Notre Dame), 27 (Fall 1996), 15–16.

In fact, only three Brazilian scholars have publicly come to Carolina's defense and argued that her writing is valuable. For years, José Carlos Sebe Bom Meihy of the University of São Paulo objected to the fact that North American academics frequently assigned the English translation of *Quarto de Despejo* to their students, saying that Carolina's depiction of favela life was increasingly outdated as conditions changed over the years, and because he felt that foreigners chose to see in Carolina's writing examples of racial and class prejudice present in their own societies as well. Brazilian intellectuals, on the whole, criticized their own society in the abstract, emphasizing theory, and were not accustomed to dealing with specifics. But in the early 1990s, after his oral history students located Carolina's surviving children and brought him into personal contact with them, Sebe radically changed his mind, coming to see Carolina as an exemplary black single mother whose life story revealed a wealth of insight into the plight of minorities, gender, and social mobility, among other issues; her unpublished plays, for example, he now argued, represented "an eloquent example of a type of culture, born in absolute poverty, that reproduces a repertory of traditional values projected into modern urban space."[7]

The second scholar to endorse Carolina's importance was UNICAMP's Marisa Lajolo, who lauded Carolina's courage in refusing to moderate her criticisms by accepting her "place." She compared Carolina's death in obscurity to the murder by police a decade later of Fernando Ramos da Silva, the boy actor who played Pixote in José Louzeiro and Hector Babenco's 1980 film of the same name.[8] The third was anthropologist Roberto DaMatta, a *carioca* on the faculty of the University of Notre Dame. Writing in his weekly column in São Paulo's *Jornal da Tarde,* DaMatta defended Carolina as a legitimate voice of "the day-to-day lives of the hungry and miserable whom we love ideologically but solemnly resent when they become successful and show themselves to be better than us." Carolina's writing, he reminds us, is all the more valuable *because* she was a black, semi-literate woman who lived by scavenging in garbage cans and who wrote to avoid losing her mind. What she produced, anthropologist DaMatta concludes, was

---

7. Letter, José Carlos Sebe Bom Meihy to Marilene Felinto, São Paulo, 30 September 1997, courtesy of J.C. Sebe Bom Meihy.

8. Marisa Lajolo, introduction to *Cinderela Negra* (Rio de Janeiro: Editora UFRJ, 1994).

extraordinarily rare: "documents revealing no less than the inner mental state of society's victims."[9]

Beyond these responses, there has been silence. The publication of additional unedited entries from Carolina's diaries in 1995 yielded several dutiful positive reviews in smaller Brazilian cities where José Carlos Sebe visited to "launch" the book, but on the whole the dismissive voices of Martins and Felinto prevailed. History textbooks published for school use in Brazil tend to fall into two camps—conservative and leftist—the former emphasizing traditional chronology and institutional history; the latter emphasizing the struggles of the underclass to assert itself against the domination of elites and foreign imperialism. Both, however, ignore one of the most eloquent witnesses of all—Carolina Maria de Jesus—perhaps because her observations did not fit formulas about who to cast as enemies.

Not only do Brazilian textbook authors in both camps fail to recognize the relevance of citing or quoting individuals from the lower classes in their observations about life, but they seem to shy away from Carolina because they are uncomfortable with her views about race, class, and patriotism. *Diário de Bitita,* the single most explicit testimonial about poverty, race prejudice, women's struggles, the role of charitable institutions, and interclass behavior during the decades of the 1920s and 1930s, has been completely and inexplicably ignored by Brazilian historians, while elite institutions such as Rio de Janeiro's CPDOC (the research and documentation center of the Getúlio Vargas Foundation) engage large numbers of archivists, historians, and staffers in collecting documents and oral histories almost exclusively from the famous and the powerful in twentieth-century Brazilian history. Other institutions that have overlooked Carolina Maria de Jesus as an important cultural figure include the research division of the Fundação Casa Rui Barbosa in Rio de Janeiro, the Center for Brazilian Studies at the University of São Paulo—which declined the offer to receive and house Carolina's private papers and personal archive, as well as several other universities and research institutes in Rio and São Paulo.

In a country such as Brazil, where as much as half of the population remains marginalized, excluded from the market economy, constrained by social mores that resist upward mobility, the manifestation of testi-

---

9. Roberto DaMatta, "Carolina, Carolina, Carolina de Jesus . . . ," *Jornal da Tarde* (São Paulo), October 11, 1996, 4.

mony from the mouth of a pariah should electrify anyone seeking to understand the past as prelude to the present. This, more than anything else, is the significance of the twenty-two autobiographical essays that comprise *Bitita's Diary*. Set in the rural interior of Brazil in the 1920s and 1930s, it offers remarkable new evidence, thick description in the phrase of Clifford Geertz, about rural life during that period. Because they were written years later—by a woman near the end of a long and harrowing life marked by fleeting success but on the whole by the pain of rejection and impoverishment—the essays lack, perhaps, the authenticity of diary entries written at the time events were taking place. But who can deny the authenticity of stories of racial prejudice within one's own family, of tense (but sometimes triumphant) relations between whites and blacks, of having to walk for miles to seek treatment for a festering illness, of the blessedness of unconditional charity, of the material deprivation of lower-class life at the onset of the Great Depression tempered by the hopes raised by Brazil's victorious 1930 Revolution?

From the perspective of the social historian, then, *Bitita's Diary* is possibly the single most riveting, and therefore most valuable, document chronicling Brazilian rural life in the early twentieth century. Like all of Carolina Maria de Jesus's writing, it is not a litany of complaint: nearly every description of cruelty and hardship is balanced, miraculously, by testimony about gratitude. Bullies taunted her for being black, for sitting under a tree and reading; her own relatives refused her food when she was starving; employers made her work for months and then never paid her; priests in Sacramento refused to let blacks worship at the town's church with whites (not only in the 1920s but down to the 1990s). But her life also contained heroes and heroines: her grandfather, born a slave, who inspired her to read; the woman who paid for her tuition at the private elementary school where she studied for two years as one of only a tiny handful of black pupils; the nuns at the hospital of the Santa Casa de Misericordia who bathed her infected sores and who treated her like a human being; Getúlio Vargas, who represented for Carolina during the early days of the 1930 Revolution a patriotic vision for her country even though she did not dare to hope that he would do much for pariahs like her.

In *Diário de Bitita,* Carolina Maria de Jesus at last realized her dream of writing about her childhood in the countryside. The book's revelations about her life in Minas Gerais were stunning, filled with nuanced detail about her experiences of poverty and racial discrimination. Some anecdotes were couched in humorous terms. For example, she described the visit of her dark-skinned uncle to a photographer's studio. The portrait came out black with only the man's white suit visible. He refused to pay, protesting "I'm not as black as that."[10] The book ends by thanking God for protecting her, even as a child, and repeating her requests from her favela days that she be permitted someday to buy a house and to live in peace.

Although the writing in *Diário de Bitita* was explicitly autobiographical, the book's Brazilian publisher, Rio de Janeiro's Nova Fronteira, classified it as fiction. Minas Gerais during the early 1920s provides the setting. There are short sections about childhood, family life, being poor, about Carolina's relatives, especially her grandfather, and about illness and work. There was even a chapter on "the rules of hospitality." The writing is chatty, precise, and clearly expressed. The book is upbeat in the same unsettling manner as *Quarto de Despejo:* statements of anger and descriptions of difficulties caused by poverty or misfortune are often followed by positive references, as if Carolina wanted to draw back from harsh judgments. "I knew my brother's father," she writes, "and I didn't know my own. Does every child have to have a father?"[11] Not only did she describe her day-to-day life, but she commented on social customs as if she were an anthropologist. Any black can be a beggar in the countryside, she explained in one comment, but in the city, the government "issued a metal tag with a number after the person was examined by a doctor and his handicap was proven."[12]

Racial identity is one of the recurrent themes in *Diário de Bitita.* Carolina devotes an entire chapter to "The Blacks." She begins by recounting a story of being caught picking fruit from a neighbor's tree. Dona Faustinha, probably a light-skinned *mulata,* confronted her, calling her a "lazy little nigger." Carolina retorted, cheekily: "Whites are thieves, too, because they stole the blacks from Africa." The neighbor looked at Carolina with "nausea." A war of insults followed, centered around Carolina's self-identification as a daughter of Africa and as a

---

10. Carolina Maria de Jesus, *Diário de Bitita* (Rio de Janeiro: Nova Fronteira, 1986), 64.

11. *Diário de Bitita,* 7.

12. *Diário de Bitita,* 27.

descendant of slaves. The narrative then turns to a discourse on work habits. Whites, Carolina asserts, are calmer than blacks because they are more economically secure.

"In 1925," she notes, "schools [in Minas for the first time] started admitting black female students. But, when the black girls came home from school, they were crying, saying they didn't want to go back to school because the whites said that the blacks smelled bad."[13] Several paragraphs attack teachers as prejudiced and lament that Brazil's abolitionists never finished their job. Then, as was her habit as a writer, she pulls back, as if afraid of offending her readers' sensibilities since national myth claimed that race discrimination did not exist. Brazil's blacks, she claims, had made great progress since abolition, citing the example of Patrício Teixeira, a samba composer, and Azevedo Costa, a black physician with his own clinic in Uberaba. Overall, though, Carolina's book offered devastating opinions about Brazilian race relations almost never seen in print. She praised Italians for hiring blacks and for letting them dance with their daughters at Saturday parties. She described black laborers who earned nine mil-réis a day but who willingly paid twice as much to sleep with white prostitutes because, in one man's words, "I always said I couldn't die without being with a white woman." "You see how the world is getting better," she quoted another: "we black men can sleep with white women now. Equality is coming."[14] She offered advice: "Blacks shouldn't kill whites. Whites shouldn't kill blacks. Blacks and whites have to dance a quadrille."[15]

Carolina, while proud of her race and African antecedents, also commonly repeated colloquial beliefs about blacks being lazy, incompetent, and prone to drunkenness. Blacks run from the police, she writes, "[like] cats running away from dogs." All of her writing was consistent in this regard: when she discussed the impact of racism on her life and the life of her family, she provided unambiguous, harrowing detail; however, when she talked about broader racial issues she lacked the intellectual and critical skills to get beyond stereotypes. Her observations about race vary between accurate commentary and gossip. *Diário de Bitita* reproduces jokes Carolina overheard spoken by old blacks commenting ruefully and with cynicism about the "nine-

---

13. *Diário de Bitita*, 38.
14. *Diário de Bitita*, 46.
15. *Diário de Bitita*, 52.

teenth-century emancipation" of blacks. Mulattos, she explains, treat blacks disdainfully because they are so proud of their lighter complexion. Black men should not impregnate white women, she observes, for "the black shouldn't produce the mulatto because he turns against him." She recounts stories of her relatives ordered out of line while waiting for water and, upon refusing, being told: "Get out of here, dirty nigger."

Carolina's frequent references in her writing to historical events affecting race relations apparently made readers nervous because she was unlettered and many of her interpretations seemed naive. Although educated Brazilians, overwhelmingly white or light-skinned, engaged the race topic frequently, many felt uncomfortable when Carolina, a black, offered details contrary to the way things were supposed to be. In *Diário de Bitita* and *Quarto de Despejo* Carolina commented on the act abolishing slavery in 1888, saying that despite legal emancipation whites still treated blacks as slaves and inferiors. She spoke passionately about Zumbi, the leader of the fugitive slave refuge at Palmares who "intended to liberate the blacks." Some of her images hit home. Blacks, she said, "silently adored Tiradentes [an advocate of Independence]." "To the blacks," she said, "he was God's minister."[16]

Carolina did not hesitate to write about the haughty and overbearing way men treated women during the period of her childhood. She wrote about the habit displayed by some males of showing their penises to women and to young girls and about other forms of sexual abuse. She observed how women feared to confront these men, taking refuge instead in deeply held religious beliefs, seeking divine intercession. Her view of the world, of course, reflected her limited education and experience. She relied on the events in her life and on aural culture. She cataloged and described the world's ostracized races through her own personal filter: blacks, hated because of their color; gypsies, hated for being thieves and wanderers without a country; and "semites," hated because they fought against Christ. Given that Jesus pardoned the Jews, she asked, why then do Christians continue to harbor resentments? When she asked an immigrant from the Middle East who was eating a *kibbe,* a cooked meat patty brought to Brazil by Arabs, whether he was a "Turk" (*turco* was the popular name for all people of Levantine origin), he replied that he was Syrian, not a Turk, and that

---

16. *Diário de Bitita,* 59.

Turks were good for nothing. She sympathized with immigrants, and laughed good-naturedly at their idiosyncrasies.

It seems remarkable that for all of the interest in twentieth-century Brazilian social history shown in Brazilian universities and among scholars around the world, *Diário de Bitita* has been consistently ignored as a vital source of information about life in rural Brazil. Hundreds of theses and dissertations have appeared during the last several decades, many of them reflecting the new importance given to women's studies and studies about race and poverty. *Diário de Bitita* offers astonishing detail about family structure, about racial prejudice, about religion (not only about the Roman Catholic Church but also about Kardecian Spiritualism, the movement that founded the primary school in which Carolina was permitted to study for two years before her mother moved her to the countryside). *Bitita* contains the only published reaction of a lower-class individual to the appearance of troops during Brazil's 1930 Revolution, and offers riveting evidence that even social pariahs welcomed Getúlio Vargas and the banners of his nationalistic movement.

Carolina's description of her dreadful treatment by her mulatto relatives when she traveled on foot to Ribeirão Preto seeking treatment at a charity hospital is one of the most poignant episodes in Brazilian writing. Her invitation to her cousins' dance, her attendance in road-stained, sweaty clothes, her hope that like Cinderella she might turn into a princess—provides astonishing reading. Her book contributes the most complete description of the curriculum of a pre-1930 small-town Brazilian primary school ever written. Her revelations about her treatment at the hands of her lighter-skinned relatives offers a treasure of nuanced information about race relations in a place where, until Carolina became famous decades after she departed from Sacramento, blacks were never permitted to attend Mass in the same church as whites.

The trajectory of Carolina's wanderings from Sacramento until she arrived in the metropolis of São Paulo persuasively documents the travails of countless tens of thousands of lower-class women driven from their places of birth by lack of opportunity for work and by the promise of a better life as domestics or industrial workers in larger cities. How many social science analyses of demography and migration lack the human side of the story recounted by Carolina Maria de Jesus?

It is true that some of Carolina's observations are likely colored by hindsight. What she wrote about Getúlio Vargas was written only after the success of his 1930 Revolution and his two-and-a-half decades in and out as head of state. Had he passed quickly from the scene, she might not have written about him when she looked back at her childhood. But her observations about Vargas are so unconventional—about the bonus in cash paid to volunteers, about how the soldiers in uniform were paraded by their mothers when they came home from military service—that we should be thankful for Carolina's memory, whether aided by hindsight or not. Her book bridges the gap between official Brazil—the Brazil of the textbooks and the accepted canon—and the genuine Brazil of the *povo,* the common people. It offers a vision of the world remarkable for what we do not expect: that a woman called a devil by those unaccustomed to seeing a black woman read came to love literature; that a woman relegated to the lowest caste could learn about the history of abolition and Brazilian politics and who Socrates was. It provides detail about life in places without any history but the pompous genealogies and lists of institutions found in dusty local historical societies throughout Brazil and its interior.

Carolina Maria de Jesus's memoirs relate misery and injustice, but she was never a bitter woman. She did not seek the fame that found her; she prayed for peace and for God's protection. To the extent that she found this, we should be thankful. We should be equally thankful for the miracle of fate that left her writings in our hands.

Robert M. Levine

About the Editor

Robert M. Levine has published seventeen books on Latin America, five of which have been translated and published there. He has chaired the Columbia University Seminar on Brazil and is past chair of the Committee on Brazilian Studies of the Conference on Latin American History. He is director of Latin American Studies at the University of Miami, Coral Gables. He was elected in 1995 a corresponding member of the Instituto Geográfico e Histórico in Rio de Janeiro. He has lectured in São Paulo, Goiânia, Natal, Rio de Janeiro, Curitiba, Recife, and Salvador. He is co-editor of the *Luso-Brazilian Review*.